Responses to 101 Questions on the Church

Richard P. McBrien

PAULIST PRESS
New York/Mahwah, N.J.

Cover design by Jim Brisson.

Scripture quotations are from the *New Revised Standard Version of the Bible*, the Division of Christian Education of the National Council of the Churches of Christ in the U.S.A. (1989). Quotations from the documents of Vatican II are taken from *The Documents of Vatican II*, America Press (1966).

Library of Congress Cataloging-in-Publication Data

McBrien, Richard P.
   Responses to 101 questions on the Church / Richard P. McBrien.
     p. cm.
   Includes bibliographical references.
   ISBN 0-8091-3638-4
    1. Church—Miscellanea. 2. Catholic Church—Doctrines—Miscellanea.
I. Title.
BX1746.M19 1996   95-26172
282—dc20   CIP

Published by Paulist Press
997 Macarthur Boulevard
Mahwah, NJ 07430

Printed and bound in the
United States of America

CONTENTS

II. *The Origins of the Church* (Questions 11-22)

III. *The Church in History* (Questions 23-37)

Contents

INTRODUCTION

I have been interested in the Church as a theological question for almost all of my adult life. During my years in the seminary, I recall reading every book and article by the French Dominican Yves Congar that I could lay my hands on. By any reasonable standard, Congar was the twentieth century's leading ecclesiologist (a theologian who specializes in the mystery and mission of the Church). He endured a great deal of criticism and misunderstanding during his lifetime, including a period of enforced silence by order of the Vatican, but his vision and work were more than vindicated by the council. In the fall of 1994, at age 90, he was named a cardinal by Pope John Paul II.

I completed my seminary studies in February 1962, just a few months before the beginning of the Second Vatican Council. After a year and a half of parish and campus ministry work in the Archdiocese of Hartford, Connecticut, I did two years of doctoral studies at the Gregorian University in Rome, during the second and third sessions of the council. A highlight of that time in Rome was a brief, but memorable, private meeting with Père Congar, who was serving as a *peritus* (or "expert") at the council. Alongside Congar, there has been no greater influence on my work as an ecclesiologist than Vatican II. Pope Paul VI pointed out at the beginning of the second session, soon after his election to the papacy, that the central question of the council was the mystery of the Church. It was the focus of almost every one of its sixteen documents: the Dogmatic Constitution on the Church *(Lumen Gentium)*, the Pastoral Constitution on the Church in the Modern World *(Gaudium et Spes)*, the Decree on Ecumenism *(Unitatis Redintegratio)*, the Declaration on the Relationship of the Church to

1

Non-Christian Religions (*Nostra Aetate*), the Decree on the Church's Missionary Activity (*Ad Gentes*), and so forth.

Soon after returning to the United States in June 1965 to join the faculty of the new Pope John XXIII National Seminary for Delayed Vocations in Weston, Massachusetts, I began writing and lecturing on my favorite theological topic by way of explaining the meaning and pastoral implications of the council. I was invited by the editor of my diocesan paper in Hartford, *The Catholic Transcript*, to do a weekly theology column, which I inaugurated in July 1966 and which is still syndicated in various Catholic newspapers. Soon thereafter my doctoral dissertation on the ecclesiology of the famous Anglican theologian and biblical scholar, Bishop John A. T. Robinson, author of the worldwide best-seller, *Honest to God* (1963), was published first in England and then in the United States, France, and Spain. An article on Robinson and the death-of-God movement, published in *Commonweal* magazine, led to an invitation from Harper & Row (now HarperCollins) to do a book which I entitled, *Do We Need the Church?* (1969). The next year, my Isaac Hecker Lectures at Wayne State University in Detroit were published by Paulist Press under the title, *Church: the Continuing Quest*.

From the outset of my life as a Catholic theologian, therefore, the mystery and mission of the Church have been at the center of my teaching, lecturing, and writing. Because ecclesiology, like moral theology, is a highly practical discipline, I have always felt that the many lectures I have given all over North America and overseas have served as a kind of global laboratory for my research and teaching. If over the years I have been able to do theology in a pastorally helpful way, it is largely because of the many thousands of questions I have been asked by people of various backgrounds, experiences, and orientations within the Church: laity, religious, priests, and even a few bishops. Like the eminent biblical scholar Father Raymond Brown, author of the first book in this *101 Questions* series, I have been struck by the frequency with which certain questions have been asked and also by the similarity of questions from place to place.

The first half of these 101 questions are really distillations of some of the thousands of questions addressed to me over the past thirty years in conferences, conventions, workshops, institutes, parishes, and classrooms alike. The second half of the book, from question 52 to the end, are actual questions, submitted in written form, by members of the audience at a Regional Adult Education and Formation Program, co-sponsored by the (Milwaukee) Archdiocesan Office of Adult and Family Ministry, the Archdiocesan Women's Commission, Sacred Heart School of Theology, and St. John Vianney Parish, Brookfield, Wisconsin, in January 1993. The theme of the conference was "Catholic Identity and the Future of the Church." Just over a year earli-er Paulist Press had contacted me to do this book, but at the time I was fully engaged with the editing of *The HarperCollins Encyclopedia* of Catholicism (published in 1995) and the revising and updating of my *Catholicism* book (published in 1994). I promised the several hundred in attendance at the Waukesha County Expo Center that some day I would try to answer most of their questions in this book, and I asked the sponsors of the program to send me copies of the questions when-ever convenient. A few months later a carefully typed, single-spaced, 15-page list of questions arrived from Betty Jean Jezo, coordinator of the Archdiocesan Women's Commission and the one who had extended the invitation and made the arrangements for my two presentations. I immediately placed the list of questions in my Paulist Press file for future use. I am happy that I have now been able to keep my word to the many members of that audience who formulated the questions, and I thank those who took the time and effort to put them together for me. Indeed, I am happy to dedicate this book to them and to Catholics like them all over the United States and Canada who devote their lives to the preaching and practice of the Gospel—with little or no compensa-tion and too often in the face of misunderstanding and even opposition. May this book assist them in their ministry and serve to reignite the fire of faith and of hope in their lives as members of the Church.

FORMAT

THE 101 QUESTIONS AND RESPONSES

Q. 1. My husband is a Methodist. Just up the street from my parish church there is a Maronite Catholic church and around the corner there's a Russian Orthodox church with an onion-shaped dome. I'm confused. When we refer to "the Church," what exactly do we mean?

In its simplest terms, the Church is the Body of Christ. It is the community of those who believe in Jesus Christ as Lord and Savior. A person becomes a member of the Church by Baptism and sustains that membership by participating actively in the Church's worship and sacramental life and, to the extent possible, in its broader ministerial endeavors on behalf of the young, the elderly, the sick, the dying, the poor, the displaced, the oppressed, and anyone else in need. This means, therefore, that *every* baptized Christian is a member of the Church, and that "the Church" is the *whole* body of Christians throughout the world, without regard for denominational differences.

Because of the circumstances of history, however, this one Church of Christ has undergone many changes, including divisions wrought by theological controversy and political conflict. Unfortunately, many Catholics tend to take a purely Western view of the Church. Non-Catholics are lumped together as Protestants, even though Anglicans (known as Episcopalians in the United States) do not regard themselves as Protestant. The only real division in the Church for such Catholics was the division created during the Protestant Reformation of the sixteenth century. Thus, we have Lutherans, Presbyterians, Baptists, Methodists, Disciples of Christ, Assemblies of

God, Dutch Reformed, and so forth. The East, meanwhile, remains shrouded in mystery, or neglected entirely.

But the division between East and West antedated the Protestant Reformation by at least five centuries. The Orthodox churches (Greek and Russian) split off from Rome at various stages, but the year 1054 is usually given as the climactic point of disruption. There are millions of Orthodox Christians spread all over the world, and particularly in Russia, Greece, the Middle East, Central and Eastern Europe, as well as in North America. The other separated non-Orthodox Oriental churches (the Assyrian, the Armenian, the Coptic, the Ethiopian, the Syrian, and the Syrian Church of India) broke from the Catholic Church as early as the fifth century when they rejected the teachings either of the Council of Ephesus in 431 or of the Council of Chalcedon in 451. The former council taught that in Jesus Christ there is only one divine person, not two, as the Nestorians held. The latter council taught that in Jesus Christ there are two natures, one human and one divine, and not only a divine nature, as the Monophysites held.

Within the Catholic Church itself, that is, within the community of churches that are in communion with the Bishop of Rome, there are several different liturgical rites: Armenian, Byzantine, Coptic, Ethiopian, East Syrian (Chaldean), West Syrian, and Maronite. Each of these rites is used in a Catholic church in communion with Rome (for example, Ukrainian, Melkite, Ruthenian, Russian, Romanian), but *none* of these is a *Roman* Catholic church. The Roman Catholic Church is one rite, also known as Latin, within the worldwide communion of Catholic churches. The Catholic Church, therefore, is neither narrowly Roman nor narrowly Western. It is universal in the fullest sense of the word.

Q. 2. If "the Church" is one, how can we speak about many "churches"?

First, because there are different denominations within the Church, as we have already indicated in the first answer. But there is another reason as well. Even in the New Testament there are references to "the Church" and then to individual "churches." The distinction here is between the universal Church and local churches. The one Church is divided, therefore, not only on the basis of denominations and liturgical rites but also on the basis of localities and regions. St. Paul, for example, recognized this fact by the way in which he began some of his letters. He addressed the Corinthians as "the church of God that is in Corinth" (1 Cor 1:2; 2 Cor 1:1), the Galatians as "the churches of Galatia" (Gal 1:2), and the Thessalonians as "the church of the Thessalonians" (1 Thess 1:1; 2 Thess 1:1). Otherwise, he used a synonym for church, such as "God's beloved in Rome, who are called to be saints" (Rom 1:7), or "the saints who are in Ephesus" (Eph 1:1), or "the saints and faithful brothers and sisters in Christ in Colossae" (Col 1:2), or "the saints in Christ Jesus who are in Philippi" (Phil 1:1).

The universal Church, that is, the worldwide Body of Christ, is composed not only of every baptized Christian but also of every individual community or denomination of Christians. The universal Church, therefore, is really a communion or college of many local churches scattered all over the globe. In Catholic theology and doctrine, each of these local churches is the Body of Christ in a particular place (Dogmatic Constitution on the Church, n. 26). The local church is not simply an administrative subdivision of the one Church, parallel to a local franchise of a fast-food chain. In every local church there is a community united by faith and Baptism. In every local church the community gathers around a eucharistic table to hear and respond to the Word of God and to eat and drink the body and blood of Christ until the Lord returns at history's end.

Q. 3. What do you mean by the term "local church"?

A parish is a local church. So, too, is a diocese. A local church could even be a regional or national grouping of parishes and dioceses. In the final analysis, the meaning of "local church" is as much a canonical question as it is theological or pastoral. In canon law, local churches are also known as "particular churches." In the more common use of the term, a particular church is a diocese, not a parish. However, theology is freer than canon law on questions like this. Theologically, a local church can mean a parish, a diocese, a regional or national grouping of parishes and dioceses, or even a denomination or patriarchate.

The smallest and most basic realization of "local church" is the parish, although in the New Testament there were even smaller units known as house churches. A diocese, in turn, is a community, or college, of parishes and similar worshiping communities within a particular geographical area. A region is a cluster of dioceses in an even larger area, and a national church is a cluster of dioceses in a particular country.

There is still one Church, which is the worldwide, or ecumenical, Body of Christ. But the one Church of Christ, from almost the very beginning of its existence, is composed of many individual churches which are, in turn, the Body of Christ in particular places.

One must take care not to exaggerate the universal Church at the expense of the local churches. We Roman Catholics have tended to do that in the past. But one must also take care not to exaggerate the individuality and autonomy of the local churches at the expense of the demands of communion with the universal Church. Some Protestants have tended to do that.

For Catholics, however, it is not an either/or matter. The Church is at once universal and local. The internal unity of each local church is sustained by a common faith in Jesus Christ, the sacraments, especially the Eucharist, the ministry of many different members, including especially the bishop, and, above all, by the active, unifying presence of the Holy Spirit. The external unity of the local churches with the universal Church is sustained by the same factors, but, in addition, by the unity of the bishops who constitute a college that represents the worldwide unity of the whole Catholic Church. The unity of the bishops is, in turn, manifested and strengthened by their unity with the Bishop of Rome, the pope. But, as in every case, it is the Holy Spirit who is the final source and guarantee of the Church's unity, whether locally or universally.

Q. 4. For what purpose does the Church exist, at whatever level?

The "purpose" of the Church's existence is also known as its "mission." Mission is derived from the Latin verb, *mittere*, which means "to send." Before the Church can be sent, however, it must first be "called." Indeed, the root meaning of the word "church" in both Hebrew (*kahal*) and Greek (*ekklesia*), from which are derived the words "ecclesial" and "ecclesiastical") is an assembly or community "called out" of the world. But the Church is "called out" for a purpose. That purpose is its mission.

The mission of the Church is that for which the Church has been called and sent—called by God the Father, sent by Jesus Christ, and empowered by the Holy Spirit. The Church's mission, therefore, can only be understood within a trinitarian framework. The Church is called and sent by the Father to carry on the work of the Son in and through the power of the Holy Spirit.

The mission of the Church can be described in various ways. There is no single, agreed-upon list of missionary tasks that belong to the Church. But surely the mission includes the proclamation of the Gospel, the celebration of the sacraments, a witnessing to Christ and the Christian faith, and service to those in need. Thus, the mission is one of word, worship, witness, and service. Sometimes you will see Greek words used to define the mission of the Church: *kerygma, leitourgia, marturia,* and *diakonia.*

The proclamation of the Gospel (word) includes preaching, catechesis, and formal teaching (for example, the work of theologians and advanced religious educators). The celebration of the sacraments has at its centerpiece the Eucharist, which the Second Vatican Council calls "the summit toward which the activity of the Church is directed...[and] the fountain from which all her power flows" (Constitution on the Sacred Liturgy, n. 10). Witnessing to Christ and the Christian faith follows from the sacramentality of the Church. In other words, the Church itself is a visible sign of the invisible presence of God in Christ. The Church must signify what it is. It must look like and act like what it claims to be, namely, the Body of Christ, the People of God, and the Temple of the Holy Spirit. Finally, the Church is committed to the service of those in need. This includes the whole of the social apostolate, that is, whatever is required by charity, justice, and mercy.

Q. 5. How do you define the Church?

I would define the Church, as I have done in my *Catholicism* book, as "the whole body, or congregation, of persons who are called by God the Father to acknowledge the Lordship of Jesus, the Son, in word, in sacrament, in witness, and in service, and, through the power of the Holy Spirit, to collaborate with Jesus' historic mission for the sake of the Kingdom of God" (San Francisco: HarperCollins, 1994, p. 723).

This definition, as one can see, embraces all Christians: Catholics (Roman and non-Roman alike), Orthodox, Anglicans, Protestants, and separated non-Orthodox Oriental Christians.

The definition also reminds us that the Church has different facets. It is, first of all, a community or a people. Second, it is an institution, because it needs the organizational and structural means to fulfill its demanding mission. Third, insofar as it collaborates with Jesus' own mission on behalf of the Kingdom, or Reign, of God, the Church is also a change-agent, servant, or liberating force in society and in history itself. Some have called these facets "models." There are, of course, many different models one might employ to describe the multifaceted nature of the Church. Jesuit theologian Avery Dulles has presented six models in the expanded edition of his well-known book, *Models of the Church* (Garden City, NY: Doubleday, 1987): institution, mystical communion, sacrament, herald, servant, and community of disciples. No one model fully captures the nature and mission of the Church. However, some models, like community of disciples or sacrament, are more fully expressive of the nature and mission of the Church than are others, for example, institution or herald.

Before all else, of course, the Church is a mystery. It is, in the words of the late Pope Paul VI given at the opening of the second session of the Second Vatican Council in 1963, "a reality imbued with the hidden presence of God." Unlike every other human organization or community, the Church is an object of faith. In the Nicene-Constantinopolitan Creed recited each Sunday at Mass, we confess our belief in the Church. But it is not the Church as an organization nor even as a people. God alone is worthy of our faith. When we say, "I believe in the Church," what we are really saying is, "I believe in the God who is present in the Church."

Q. 6. The definition, you said, includes all Christians. But how would you define the "Catholic" Church?

The Catholic Church—which, again, includes both Roman and non-Roman Catholics—is that particular community of Christians within the worldwide Body of Christ whose unity with Christ and with one another is rooted not only in the Holy Spirit, faith in Christ, the sacraments, and a common commitment to the Christian life, but also, and uniquely, in the Petrine ministry exercised by the Bishop of Rome, better known as the pope.

That's the simplest and most direct way of differentiating the Catholic Church within the whole Body of Christ, namely, by focusing on the successor of Peter. Catholics alone recognize the pope as having special pastoral and ministerial authority over the whole Church, an authority derived from Christ's mandate to Peter: "And I tell you, you are Peter, and on this rock I will build my church, and the gates of Hades will not prevail against it. I will give you the keys of the kingdom of heaven, and whatever you bind on earth will be bound in heaven, and whatever you loose on earth will be loosed in heaven" (Matt 16:18-19).

But to understand the "Catholic" Church, one must understand the meaning of "Catholicism" itself. Catholicism is a rich and diverse reality. It is a Christian tradition, a way of life, and a community of faith. It's not just one of these; it's all three. The word "Catholic" is derived from the Greek adjective, *katholikos*, which means "universal," and from the Greek adverbial phrase, *kath' holou*, which means "on the whole."

Some people think that the opposite of "Catholic" is "Protestant." It's not. The opposite of "Catholic" is "sectarian." A sect is a part of the Church that has separated itself off from the worldwide Church and even, to some extent, from the world itself. A sect closes itself off from others in order to maintain its own identity and purity. Contact with the outside world, even contact with other Christians outside the sect, is regarded as contaminating.

In the fifth century the great St. Augustine of Hippo contrasted the separatist and sectarian movements of his time, especially Donatism in North Africa, with the Catholic Church that is both universal and orthodox in its faith. The Donatists, he said, existed only in a small part of the world, while the Catholic Church is spread over the whole world, in all those places where the apostles have brought the Gospel of Jesus Christ. St. Cyril of Jerusalem, in the previous century, had been even more explicit about the meaning of Catholicism. "The Church is called 'Catholic'," he insisted, "because it extends through all the world...because it teaches universally and without omission all the doctrines which ought to come to human knowledge...because it brings under the sway of true religion all classes of people, rulers and subjects, learned and ignorant; and because it universally treats and cures every type of sin...and possesses in itself every kind of virtue which can be named...and spiritual gifts of every kind" (*Catechetical Lectures*, 18.23).

The use of the word "Catholic" to define the Church became divisive after the East-West Schism of the eleventh century and the Protestant Reformation of the sixteenth. The West claimed for itself the title "Catholic Church," while the separated East appropriated the name "Holy Orthodox Church." After the Reformation, supporters of the papacy retained the name "Catholic," while the churches that broke with Rome were called "Protestant." But there are many non-Catholic Christian churches that believe themselves to be reformed, evangelical, *and* Catholic all at the same time. The Second Vatican Council seemed to be reaching out to them when it broadened the notion of catholicity to include churches outside the Catholic Church (Dogmatic Constitution on the Church, n. 8) and referred to them as possessing varying "degrees" of catholicity (Decree on Ecumenism, n. 3).

Q. 7. Do we still speak of the marks of the Church today?

There are traditionally four marks, or notes, of the Church: unity, holiness, catholicity, and apostolicity. These four marks are drawn from the Nicene-Constantinopolitan Creed (more popularly known as the Nicene Creed) that is recited each week at the Eucharist: "We believe in one holy catholic and apostolic Church." Emphasis on the marks of the Church came about during the period of inter-church controversy following the Protestant Reformation. With so many different churches vying for recognition and making various claims for themselves, defenders of the Catholic faith, known as apologists, appealed to the four marks in order to distinguish the true Church from the false churches. The supposition was that the marks would be visible to all and easy to verify, and that they would be present only in the one, true Church of Christ. The problem was that the description of the notes tended to be drawn in such a way that they would fit the Catholic Church, and the Catholic Church alone. Thus, a Catholic apologist would include in his definition of the unity of the Church the requirement that the universal Church must be united under the earthly head-ship and pastoral authority of the pope. No matter what was said about any of the other three marks of the Church, the mark of unity, thus described, would automatically eliminate every other church's claim to being the true Church of Christ. A second difficulty with the apologeti-cal approach was its assumption that the marks of the Church described fully the way the Church is, even now. But the Church of Christ is divided, not fully united. It is still marred by sin. It is not totally faithful to the apostolic word and witness. It still lacks complete and total openness to all truth, such as catholicity demands.

A more recent approach to the marks of the Church is to view them less apologetically and more eschatologically. What does that mean? It means that the marks are not so much proofs of the claims of the Catholic Church as they are aspects of, or insights into, the mystery of the Church, Catholic and non-Catholic alike. The marks are also goals to be realized. Thus, we say today that the Church is one, but not yet fully one. It must overcome divisions and achieve full communion. The Church is holy, but not yet fully holy. It must struggle against its own sinfulness and follow always the path of penance and renewal. The Church is catholic, but not yet fully catholic. It must open itself even more to the diverse peoples of the world and to truth wherever it is to be found. The Church is apostolic, but not yet fully apostolic. It must strive to become even more faithful to the message and mission it has received from the apostles. Not until the Second Coming of Christ and the final manifestation of the Reign of God will the oneness, holi-ness, catholicity, and apostolicity of the Church be complete.

Nevertheless, the unity of the Church is already present in the Eucharist and through the various ministries that are dedicated to the service of unity. The holiness of the Church is already present in the grace of the Holy Spirit who animates each member and the whole community. The catholicity of the Church is already present in the Church's outreach to the whole world and to its active presence in all the nations of the world. The apostolicity of the Church is already pre-sent in the apostolic word that is preached, worship that is offered, wit-ness that is given, and service that is rendered to those in need.

Q. 8. Is the Catholic Church still to be considered as the "one, true Church" of Christ?

Yes, if by "one, true Church" we mean that the Catholic Church alone is lacking nothing of what Christ and the Apostles intended for the Church; for example, the seven sacraments, especially the Eucharist, and the Petrine ministry exercised by the pope as Bishop of Rome. Other churches, however, have a "certain, though imperfect, communion with the Catholic Church" (Decree on Ecumenism, n.3). No, if by "one, true Church" we mean that the Catholic Church and the Body of Christ are one and the same; in other words, that the Catholic Church is the only real Church and that all other churches are essentially "false churches" which are outside the Body of Christ.

The Second Vatican Council's Dogmatic Constitution on the Church (*Lumen Gentium*) gives support to both answers. The Catholic Church is the "one, true Church" in that it lacks nothing that is essential to the Body of Christ: "They are fully incorporated into the society of the Church who, possessing the Spirit of Christ, accept its entire system and all the means of salvation given it, and through union with its visible structure are joined to Christ, who rules it through the Supreme Pontiff and the bishops" (n. 14).

On the other hand, the Catholic Church is not the "one, true Church" in the sense that Catholics alone are in the Body of Christ: "This Church, constituted and organized in the world as a society, subsists in the Catholic Church, which is governed by the successor of Peter and by the bishops in union with that successor, although many elements of sanctification and of truth can be found outside of its visible structure" (n. 8). This is one of the most discussed passages in all of the council documents. The verb "subsists in" replaced the verb "is" in the final draft of the Dogmatic Constitution. The change was significant. The copulative verb "is" would have equated the Catholic Church and the Body of Christ. The verb "subsists in" was intended to show that other churches are also in the Body of Christ.

Q. 9. Is the Church necessary for salvation?

The answer is "Yes," but that's the easy part. Explaining *why* it's "Yes" is more difficult. Because the Church is the Body of Christ, it embodies the presence of Christ and carries on his redemptive work for all of humanity. In that sense, the Church is indeed necessary for salvation, that is, in the same way that Jesus Christ himself is necessary for salvation. But does that mean that only those who profess faith in Jesus Christ as Lord and Savior can be saved?

Jesus himself gave us the beginning of an answer to both questions when he said, "Not everyone who says to me, 'Lord, Lord,' will enter the kingdom of heaven, but only the one who does the will of my Father in heaven" (Matt 7:21). Confessing the Lordship of Jesus, therefore, isn't in itself sufficient for salvation. But even if it's not sufficient, is it absolutely necessary? Later in the twenty-fifth chapter of Matthew's Gospel Jesus narrates the parable of the sheep and the goats in which he implies that many who enter the kingdom of heaven will not even have been aware of the Lord. Rather, they will only encounter the Lord anonymously, as it were, in the hungry, the thirsty, the homeless, and all others in need.

Catholic belief and teaching about salvation, therefore, is that no one is saved apart from the redemptive work of Jesus Christ on behalf of all humanity, but that it is possible to be the beneficiary of that redemptive work even if one does not confess Jesus as Lord and Savior, which means even if one is not a member of the Church, Catholic or non-Catholic.

That wasn't always the understanding of the Church's role in salvation, however. In the first three centuries the saying, "No salvation outside the Church," was used exclusively as a warning against Christians who had separated themselves from the Church by heresy or schism. Historians have found no instance where that same warning was issued against the pagan majority in the Roman Empire. It was only after Christianity became the official religion of the Empire in the fourth century that the saying began to be applied to Jews and pagans as well. The naive assumption was that, by this time, the Gospel had been preached to the whole world. Those who still had not accepted it were culpable and, therefore, heading for damnation. This was the view associated especially with Fulgentius, bishop of Ruspe, in the sixth century, and it remained standard Catholic teaching for almost a thousand years. The Council of Florence in 1442 used Fulgentius' formula in its own teaching. With the discovery of America, however, only fifty years after

Florence, it became clear that the world was much larger than had been thought. There were still many thousands—perhaps millions—of people who had never heard of Jesus Christ. Only gradually thereafter did the hard-line teaching of Fulgentius and others yield to a broader, more ecumenical view of salvation outside the Church.

At first, a distinction was made between members of the Church *in re* (that is, actual, baptized members) and members of the Church *in voto* (that is, people of good will who remain outside the Church through no fault of their own). All those who are saved are saved because of some relationship with the Church, whether *in re* or *in voto*. The Second Vatican Council went a step beyond that position. It recognized in its Decree on Ecumenism that non-Catholic churches are a "means of salvation," although "they derive their efficacy from the fullness of grace and truth entrusted to the Catholic Church" (n. 3). The council also recognized in its Declaration on the Relationship of the Church to Non-Christian Religions that the "Catholic Church rejects nothing which is true and holy in these religions" (n. 2).

Does the Church, then, play any necessary role at all in the salvation of the world? Yes, says the council, it is the "universal sacrament of salvation" (Dogmatic Constitution on the Church, n. 48; Pastoral Constitution on the Church in the Modern World, n. 45; Decree on the Church's Missionary Activity, n. 1). Not only are all peoples related to the Church by the grace which the Holy Spirit offers them, but the Church itself is a sign and instrument of their salvation. And that is the newer, more ecumenical, more universal meaning of the traditional saying, "No salvation outside the Church."

Q. 10. You say that Catholicism is a rich and diverse reality. I thought Catholicism is the same all over the world. How can it be "diverse"?

Catholicism is distinguished within the Body of Christ by its understanding of, commitment to, and particular stress upon certain key Christian principles. Included among these are the principles of sacramentality, mediation, and communion.

It is no accident that the sacraments are so central a part of Catholic faith and life. Catholicism is, at its core, a sacramental tradition. It "sees" God in all things, as St. Ignatius of Loyola, founder of the Jesuits, was fond of saying. It sees the divine in the human, the infinite in the finite, the spiritual in the material, the eternal in the temporal. For Catholicism, therefore, all reality is sacred. Everything is actually or at least potentially a carrier and instrument of the divine glory. Nowhere is this sacramental vision more sharply focused than on Jesus Christ himself, for he is the great sacrament of our encounter with God and of God's with us. The Church, in turn, is the sacrament of our encounter with Christ and of Christ's with us. And the seven sacraments, in their turn, are sacraments of our encounter with the Church and of the Church's with us. Indeed, the other members of the Church are sacraments of encounter for us and we for them because, in the Christian scheme of things, we experience and manifest the love of God through love of neighbor.

For Catholicism, therefore, the world is essentially good, although fallen, because it comes from the creative hand of God, has been redeemed by Jesus Christ, and has been renewed by the power and presence of the Holy Spirit. Human existence is graced existence. The history of the world is, at the same time, the history of salvation.

Mediation is a second major principle that finds particular emphasis and embodiment in the Catholic tradition. A sacrament, after all, not only signifies; it also causes what it signifies. Catholicism insists that the human encounter with God and God's encounter with humanity is always a mediated encounter. God uses human and material instruments to provide a bridge between the divine and the human. Jesus Christ and the Church are, for Catholics, the great bridges between heaven and earth. Even the imperial title which popes still use highlights this point. The pope is referred to as the "Supreme Pontiff." The word "pontiff" is derived from the Latin, *pons*, which means "bridge," and *facere*, which means "to make" or "to build." The pontiff is, literally, a bridge-builder.

The principle of mediation is especially apparent in the use of sacraments, sacramentals (crucifixes, holy water, statues, paintings, medals, rosaries, ashes, palms, and so forth), and other prayers and rituals which are designed to bridge the gap between the spiritual and the material, the sacred and the secular, the supernatural and the natural. The principle is also at work in the ministry of priests and other ministers of the Church. And nowhere is the Catholic dimension of the

nciple more obviously engaged than in Catholicism's
Mary intercedes for us. In cooperation with her Son, and
linate to him, Mary brings us to God and God to us.

nciple of communion, finally, emphasizes that our way to
God and God's way to us, while always personal and individual, is also
always and essentially communal. We are saved not only as individual
persons but as a people. After all, in the sin of Adam and Eve all of us,
not just Adam and Eve, fell from the grace of God. And in the redemptive work of Christ, all of us, as a whole people, were restored to the
good graces of God. This is why the mystery of the Church has always
had such a significant place in Catholic theology, doctrine, and pastoral
practice. The Church is the sacrament of what God is, in fact, doing on
behalf of all. It is that special community wherein God and humanity
spiritually and materially interact for the salvation of the whole world.

Q. 11. Was Jesus the founder of the Church?

Yes and No. Yes, Jesus was the founder of the Church if by
"founder" you mean the one who inaugurated the Christian movement
within the Judaism of his day by calling disciples, by sending them
forth among the Jewish people "to proclaim the kingdom of God and
to heal" (Luke 9:2), and by establishing a table fellowship by which his
disciples would remain together after his death. Indeed, he had
enjoined his disciples at the Last Supper, "Do this in remembrance of
me" (1 Cor 11:24). Likewise, his words to Simon Peter suggest that the
disciples understood Jesus as having intended them to stay together:
"Simon, Simon, listen! Satan has demanded to sift all of you like
wheat, but I have prayed for you that your own faith may not fail; and
you, when you have turned back, strengthen your brothers" (Luke
22:31-32). In fact, there was never a churchless period in the New
Testament following the resurrection of Jesus.

No, Jesus was not the founder of the Church if by "founder" you
mean the one who formally and deliberately began a new religious
community, separate from Judaism, with its own doctrines, rituals,
sacraments, ethical code, and organizational structure. He said, in fact,
that his mission was not to gather together all of the just and the right-
eous. He even instructed his disciples to go "nowhere among the

Gentiles, and enter no town of the Samaritans, but go rather to the lost sheep of the house of Israel" (Matt 10:5-6).

It has been the traditional belief of Catholics that Jesus founded the Church when he called the Twelve Apostles, representing the twelve tribes of Israel, and sent them out to preach the Gospel to the whole world in order to "make disciples of all nations, baptizing them in the name of the Father and of the Son and of the Holy Spirit, and teaching them to obey everything" that he had commanded them (Matt 28:19-20).

We should not be surprised, however, to find no evidence of any specific act of founding a Church. Had Jesus done so, his action would have been interpreted as the founding of a separate synagogue and would have minimized or even destroyed the uniqueness of his message. The oft-quoted reference to the founding of a Church in Matthew 16:18 ("...you are Peter, and on this rock I will build my church...") is, in fact, the only such reference. Not until Jesus had risen from the dead do the first Christians even speak of a "Church."

A final reason why the evidence is not there is that Jesus most probably expected the Kingdom of God to come very soon—at first within his own lifetime and then, as the delay of its coming became clearer to him, sometime soon after his death. Why, then, would Jesus have intended to found an entirely new religious institution, distinct from Judaism, if he thought the world was about to come to an end?

In summary, Jesus emerges from the pages of the New Testament as a Jewish rabbi, a prophet, and an itinerant preacher who spoke with unusual authority because he was convinced of his intensely close relationship to God and of the mission which God had given him to proclaim the nearness of the Kingdom of God and of its presence through himself. By gathering disciples and by providing for a continued discipleship in the real and symbolic meal that was the Last Supper, he at least laid the foundations for the Church. But this is not to say that Jesus intended a religious movement separate from Judaism.

Q. 12. Did Jesus ordain the Twelve Apostles at the Last Supper and then instruct them to hand on their apostolic powers to successors?

The answer to both parts of the question is "No." There is no biblical or historical evidence for the assumptions that there were ordinations at the Last Supper and that Jesus laid down instructions for the process of apostolic succession. This is not to say that the Last Supper was an event of minimal importance. On the contrary, it was one of the most significant in the life of Jesus and his disciples. It was at this meal, as pointed out in the response to the previous question, that Jesus sought to insure the continuation of the community of his disciples beyond his own death. In that respect, his injunction, "Do this in remembrance of me," has been traditionally understood as one of several positive indicators of his intention to launch a new religious movement, which only later came to be known as "the Church."

It is also worth recalling the significance of such meals for the contemporary culture. Sharing a meal signified a bond of unity, even a sharing of one's life. In Judaism, table fellowship implied fellowship with God. So when Jesus took meals with his disciples, particularly his final meal with them, it was his way of reaching out to embrace the people of God in the heavenly banquet. He said on this occasion, "Truly I tell you, I will never again drink of the fruit of the vine until that day when I drink it new in the kingdom of God" (Mark 14:25). What is equally important is that when Jesus took meals with those whom society regarded as unclean or unworthy, such as tax collectors, he was also making a statement about the inclusiveness of God's kingdom. God welcomes everyone, regardless of their station or situation in life. Only the self-righteous and the hard-of-heart are excluded—by their own behavior.

But as significant as the Last Supper was, there is no evidence that any ordination ceremony took place there. None of the New Testament accounts refers to a laying on of hands. Moreover, nowhere in the whole of the New Testament—not just at the Last Supper—is there any reference to the Twelve Apostles' appointing others as their successors or to their laying hands on others in order to constitute them officially as their successors.

When Judas died, he was replaced by Matthias, upon the casting of lots (Acts 1:26). Significantly, after the execution of James, the son of Zebedee, around the year 62, James was not replaced, indicating that the role of the Twelve had diminished as the mission of the Church extended beyond Jerusalem to the Gentiles.

Consequently, if we are to maintain our traditional Catholic belief in the ordained priesthood and in apostolic succession—and indeed we should—it has to be on some basis other than the New Testament. The most obvious alternative is the teaching of the Church. The Council of Trent (1545-63) firmly taught these doctrines over against the Protestant Reformers of the day, who, in effect, asserted that priestly ordination and the apostolic succession of bishops were contrary to the will of Christ. Trent rejected that view. On the other hand, it used various biblical arguments to buttress its position. By present standards of biblical scholarship, fully endorsed and even actively promoted by the hierarchical magisterium of the Church, those scriptural arguments do not support the doctrinal conclusions. That does not mean, however, that the conclusions are wrong.

Q. 13. Even if, as you say, Jesus did not regard his community of disciples as a religious movement separate from Judaism, didn't the early Church think of itself as a new religion?

It depends, of course, by what we mean by "early Church." If we're talking about the Church of the first century, the answer is "No." From the 30s to the 60s, for example, Jesus' disciples expected him to return and the world to end in the very near future. Indeed, because they still considered themselves Jews, they continued their Jewish practices, meeting in homes for prayer, teaching, and reflection on the sayings of Jesus. Many of the early Christians also observed the Law, attended the temple, and seemed to have no concern for the Gentiles.

According to New Testament scholars, there were four basic positions in the early Church regarding the relationship between the fledgling Christian movement and Judaism. The first position was that of Jewish Christians and their Gentile converts who insisted on the full observance of the Mosaic law, including circumcision (in fact, they were even called the "circumcision party" and Paul referred to them as "false brethren"). The second group of Jewish Christians and Gentile converts did not insist on circumcision but required Gentile converts to observe some of the Jewish purity laws (this group included Peter and James, the brother of the Lord). The third group of Jewish Christians and Gentile converts also did not insist on circumcision, but neither did they require Gentile converts to observe Jewish dietary laws (a position held by Paul himself). The fourth group of Jewish Christians and Gentile converts insisted neither on circumcision nor on Jewish dietary laws and also saw no lasting significance in Jewish worship, in the temple and on feasts (this was the position of the Hellenists, which included Stephen, Philip, and the rest of the Seven, popularly known as deacons).

These tensions came to a boil at an assembly known as the Council of Jerusalem, held around 49 or 50 A.D. We can't easily exaggerate the significance of this meeting. It challenges some of our most cherished assumptions about the Church's structure, particularly as it applies to the papacy. First, the council was presided over by James, not by Peter. Second, at this council the ultra-conservative "circumcision party," known also as the Judaizers, openly opposed Peter, whom tradition identifies as the first pope. Third, a pastoral solution based on practical considerations and on compromise rather than on fixed doctrine was agreed upon under James' leadership. The Gentile converts were not to be required to undergo circumcision, but they were encouraged to abstain from foods that might otherwise offend their Jewish Christian brothers and sisters.

It is significant that, even at the end of the New Testament period (already into the second century), there was no universal agreement among Christians on the relationship between the Church and Judaism. Therefore, it wasn't something evident to all of the early Christians that Jesus had indeed founded a new Church separate from Judaism and that he had clearly intended his disciples to break their connection with Judaism, once and for all, lock, stock, and barrel. The issue is simply far more complicated than that.

Q. 14. Was Peter the first pope and did he have immediate successors?

According to the long-standing tradition and practice of the Catholic Church, the pope is one and the same with the Bishop of Rome. Therefore, the question can be put another way: Was Peter the first Bishop of Rome and did he have immediate successors in that office?

The problem is that Peter came to Rome sometime after the Christian faith and the Church were planted there (probably in the early 40s). Paul's Letter to the Romans, which provides our best evidence regarding the state of the Church in Rome at this time, suggests that Peter did not have any significant association with the Roman church before the year 58, and it may be that he came to Rome only in the early 60s. Was he the pope before he arrived in Rome? Traditional Catholic belief holds that he was. If so, it cannot be said that the papacy is essentially linked with Rome for all time, because Peter wasn't even in Rome until more than two decades after the death and resurrection of Jesus. Furthermore, there is no historical evidence whatever that the so-called monoepiscopal structure of church governance was operative in Rome throughout the whole of the first century. Indeed, even by the mid-80s there is no evidence that any one individual functioned in the Petrine role for the universal Church, either at Antioch or anywhere else, including Rome.

Most scholars agree that the popes listed after Peter—Linus, Anacletus, Clement, and so forth—did not function as bishops of Rome in the sense in which we understand the word "bishop" today. Rome seems to have been governed instead by a committee or board of pastoral leaders. Perhaps Linus and the others functioned as chairmen or conveners of the board. Indeed, when Ignatius of Antioch (d. ca. 107) wrote his letters to various churches in Asia Minor and at Rome, his letter to Rome is the only one in which he fails to mention a bishop who is head of the local community. In any case, not until the pontificate of Pius I (ca. 142–ca. 155) do we have our first clear indication of a single bishop functioning as the pastoral leader of Rome.

Does all this mean that the traditional Catholic belief in the papacy is without warrant? No. It only means that some traditional Catholic assumptions about the papacy are questionable at best. Clearly, the office of pope has evolved over the centuries. Catholics and others have to be careful not to read back into the earliest decades and centuries of the Church what we take for granted about the papacy today. Any resemblance, therefore, between Pope John Paul II, who has been so dominant a papal figure during the final decades of the twentieth century, and Pope Pius I, for example, would be purely coincidental. And the papacy of the late fortieth century will probably look even more different from today's papacy than the papacy of the late twentieth century looks in relationship to that of the first or second centuries.

Q. 15. Were there bishops in the early Church?

Yes. And in light of some of the previous answers, you're probably a little relieved to hear it. But once again we need to pause and reflect on the crucial matter of historical development. To say that there were bishops in the early Church is not to say that every church in the earliest decades of the Christian era had bishops (Corinth, for example, did not), nor is it to say that the bishops that did exist were exactly like the bishops Catholics are familiar with today.

The principal source for our knowledge and understanding of the development of the Church in the 50s and early 60s is the Pauline letters. But even they don't give us a full picture of the Church in their period, because, for the most part, they were written in response to specific pastoral needs and situations. It is significant, however, that Paul never mentions presbyters or elders (today's "priests") in any of his letters, and that he mentions bishops (*episkopoi* in the Greek, meaning "overseers") and deacons only in Philippians 1:1. Although ministerial roles and pastoral offices were widely varied at this time, at least three seem to have been operative in the Church of the 50s: apostles (that is, missionary leaders in contrast to local, residential leaders), fellow workers (patrons and protectors, evangelists, instructors of the faith), and local leaders (some of these overlapped with "fellow workers"). There were no cultic leaders who were called "priests." Indeed, there are only two specific references to the Eucharist in Paul's undisputed letters (both references in First Corinthians), and nowhere in any of his letters does he say anything about who presided at these meals.

The real turning-point for the early Church came from the early 60s to the end of the 70s, a segment of time known as the sub-apostolic period. The principal leaders of the Church (Peter, Paul, James) had been martyred, the Temple and the city of Jerusalem had been destroyed by the Romans (in the year 70), and it was obvious to most that the Lord's Second Coming was to be further delayed. The torch of church leadership passed from Jewish Christians to Gentile Christians, and from the city of Jerusalem to other important cities in the Roman Empire: Antioch, Alexandria, and especially Rome, referred to in Ignatius of Antioch's letter to the Romans as "preeminent in love."

The office of bishop developed outside of Jewish Christian regions (which reflected the synagogue model of governance), in

Greek-speaking territories, and in response to particular pastoral problems that required a special kind of pastoral leadership. The principal
problem was that of false teachers (Titus 1:10-11; 1 Tim 4:1-2; 2 Tim
3:6) and the confusion resulting from the spread of their teachings. It
was thought that the most effective way to combat this new scourge
was through strong pastoral leadership: that of the supervisors, or overseers (bishops), and elders (presbyters). In many instances in the early
Church, these two offices weren't even distinct. There were presbyter-
bishops as well as just plain bishops and just plain presbyters. By contrast, however, the Johannine communities showed no interest in such
offices. Discipleship, not pastoral authority, was the dominant value.
For the Johannine Christians, the unity of the Church is preserved, not
by apostolic succession, but by Jesus himself through the working of
the Holy Spirit, or Paraclete. But openness to the Spirit was not without its own difficulties and risks. Bitter disputes broke out within these
very Johannine communities (1 John 1:3; 2:19; 4:1.6).

Q. 16. How did the early Church organize itself for its mission?

The first point that has to be made, as should be evident from the
previous answer, is that there is no uniform order or structure in the
Church of the New Testament. Some local churches were guided by
presbyters, others had overseers, or bishops (Acts 20:28). There was
great variety from place to place. We don't know, for example, how the
Twelve Apostles functioned in the original church community in
Jerusalem, and why they receded into the background after they gathered the community of disciples together to resolve the conflict
between spiritual and administrative duties (Acts 6:2), or what rank or
position the seven men had who were selected to "wait on tables"
(Acts 6:3-6). Were they, in fact, the first deacons? While there is no
doubt that Peter held a position of prominence, we are less sure about
James, the "brother of the Lord," who assumed a role of pastoral leadership in Jerusalem alongside Peter (Acts 12:17; 15:13-21; Gal 1:19;
2:9) and after Peter left (Gal 2:12; Acts 21:18).

On the other hand, there was never a time when the Church of the
New Testament was without at least *some* order and structure. While
there was a radical equality in the community of disciples, based on

their common humanity and Baptism (Gal 3:28), there was also a differentiation of ministries and charisms and a gradation of offices in the fulfillment of the Church's mission (1 Cor 12:4-11). There is mention, first, of the Apostles, then of prophets, evangelists, pastors, and teachers "to equip the saints for the work of ministry, for building up the body of Christ" (Eph 4:11-12). Paul called upon Christians to respect "those who labor among you, and have charge of you in the Lord and admonish you..." (1 Thess 5:12). Indeed, there is a sacred order of ministers and pastors who are responsible to their heavenly chief shepherd "to tend the flock of God that is in [their] charge, exercising the oversight..." (1 Pet 5:2-4). Paul himself exercised such authority. Despite his absence from Corinth, it was he who decided the case of the incestuous man (1 Cor 5:3-5), gave directives for the divine service (11:17,33), rendered admonishments and concrete prescriptions (7:17; 16:1; Titus 1:5), and made definitive moral judgments (1 Thess 4:11; 2 Thess 3:4,6,10,12). Certainly the Church at Corinth recognized Paul's apostolic authority because they submitted questions to him for decision (1 Cor 7:1).

Peter, of course, had a unique place in this emerging structure. He is the most frequently mentioned disciple in all four Gospels. He functioned as the spokesman of the Apostles and is always placed first on lists of Apostles (Matt 10:2). It was Peter who took the decisive step in ordering the baptism of the Gentile Cornelius (Acts 10), thus precipitating a major pastoral crisis that culminated in the council of Jerusalem (Acts 15), and his influence in Gentile areas is obvious (1 Cor 1:12; 1 Pet 1:1).

Q. 17. When did the present system of bishops, priests, and deacons begin?

Certainly by the end of the second century. However, already by the end of the first century and the beginning of the second (known as the post-apostolic period), the organizational structure of the Church, of a type familiar to present-day Catholics, began to take shape. The Church saw itself by this time as a religious body distinct from Judaism. It viewed the Eucharist now as an unbloody sacrifice that replaced the sacrifices offered in the Temple. Those who presided at the Eucharist were soon called priests, although in the beginning only bishops were spoken of as offering sacrifice. There was also a growing tendency to situate church officials within a divinely ordered pattern of the universe and the ordered structure of the imperial government. Clement, traditionally regarded as the fourth pope, drew exact parallels with the imperial system, insisting that church leaders commanded the same obedience as military and civil authorities.

In Antioch, where Ignatius was bishop, there was a clear distinction among the three ordained ministries of bishop, priest (presbyter), and deacon. As the author of the Pastoral Letters of the New Testament (Titus and 1 and 2 Timothy) had done, Ignatius emphasized the role of pastoral leadership, especially that of the bishop, to combat various challenges to the unity and doctrinal integrity of the Church: a Judaizing movement in theology and worship, Docetism and Gnosticism (two anti-body heresies that tore the early Church apart), and persecution. Ignatius' structure was monoepiscopal and tripartite: one bishop per diocese; three ordained ministries. At the same time, however, there was still no clear distinction between presbyters and bishops in Rome. Instead, there were presbyter-bishops and deacons, as in the Pastoral Letters. Indeed, scholars remind us that the organizational shift that occurred at Antioch should not be exaggerated, because the Christian community there was probably no bigger than a large modern-day parish, with the bishop serving, in effect, as its pastor.

To be sure, the monoepiscopal structure and the tripartite system of ordained ministry have been an integral part of Catholic doctrine and practice from almost the very beginning of the Church's existence, and certainly by the end of the second century they had become the norm. Given the variations within this early history, however, it is clear that the Church has ample freedom to adapt and to modify these organizational structures and systems in response to new and unforeseen pastoral challenges—just as those structures and systems were developed in the first place in response to such challenges.

Q. 18. What kind of authority did Jesus give his Apostles and their successors?

Whatever authority Jesus conferred upon the Apostles and their successors, it was not identical with his own. Not even Peter, the chief

of the Apostles, received the absolute authority which only Jesus, as
the Son of God, possessed. In the Acts of the Apostles, chapters 1-12,
where Peter's leadership is most clearly portrayed, important decisions
are made by "the Twelve" or "the apostles" or "the church," and not by
Peter alone. His actions are reviewed critically by "the circumcised
believers" (11:1-18). He is openly rebuked by Paul for his devious
behavior at Antioch (Gal 2:11-14). Peter had been eating with the
Gentiles, contrary to Jewish law, but then stopped when some conservative Jewish Christians came to town.

As a group the Apostles themselves were not the sole participants in Jesus' authority. There were also prophets, teachers, wonder-
workers, evangelists, presbyters, and others (1 Cor 12:28; Eph 4:11).
Paul himself was harshly and unjustly criticized by some of the
Corinthians, but he responded with warmth, never suggesting that he
was above criticism because of his apostolic status. Indeed, it was
clearly understood that the Holy Spirit was given to the whole Church
and not just to its pastoral leaders (1 Cor 12:1-28; Rom 12:3-8). There
is a diversity of gifts and charisms. All must work together as one for
the good of the whole.

Q. 19. Did the bishops have teaching authority from the beginning?

Yes, but not exclusively. "Teacher" was a common category in
the New Testament. It applied even to the Scribes. Jesus himself was a
teacher, and was regarded as such. He explained the nature of the
Kingdom of God and its moral demands. People were amazed by what
he said and by the depth of authority with which he said it.

The New Testament, however, conceives of the Gospel and the
Christian faith primarily as a way of life, not a teaching. Only in
Matthew are the Apostles commissioned to teach, which may help
explain why biblical scholars refer to that Gospel as the most Jewish of
the four. When the Apostles did teach, their object was Christ (Acts
5:42), the word of the Lord (15:35), the word of God (18:11), the person and mission of Christ (Colossians), and the Second Coming of
Christ (2 Thessalonians). Significantly, when teaching is enumerated

among the gifts of the Holy Spirit, it is listed *after* revelation, knowledge, and prophecy (1 Cor 14:6).

At Antioch there were prophets and teachers (Acts 13:1). Teachers were listed with other officers of the Church (Rom 12:7; 1 Cor 12:28; Eph 4:11). They explained the person and mission of Jesus Christ and the demands of discipleship in light of the Old Testament. But teachers did not constitute an elite or superior group within the Church, as the Scribes were within contemporary Judaism. Nor was teaching limited to certain persons. It was only as the Church grew and its organizational structure became more complex that concerns were expressed about doctrinal deviations and unsound teaching (1 Tim 1:3-7; 6:2-5; 2 Tim 4:3-4; Titus 1:9-14; 3:9).

The primary function of the Church in the New Testament was not teaching, but evangelization, that is, the proclamation of the Gospel, the announcement of the good news of the Kingdom of God. Teaching was the explanation of the Gospel, not its proclamation. As such, teaching was an important subsidiary function done by church members whom we would call today theologians and religious educators. In the Middle Ages, for example, St. Thomas Aquinas distinguished between the teaching authority exercised by the bishops and the teaching authority exercised by the theologians.

Q. 20. What pastoral or ministerial roles did women play in the early Church?

There is no evidence that women functioned as bishops or priests (presbyters), but there are indications that women may have exercised the ministry of the diaconate.

The classic text, of course, is Galatians 3:27-28: "As many of you as were baptized into Christ have clothed yourselves with Christ. There is no longer slave or free, there is no longer male and female; for all of you are one in Christ Jesus." The Church of the New Testament period was convinced that by Baptism every member of the Church is equal before God and has equal access to salvation. Although Paul's primary point here was to underscore the equality of Jews and Gentiles, his insistence on the equality of male and female is nevertheless of great significance.

At the time of Paul (50s and early 60s) some women were very prominent in the church communities. Prisca and her husband Aquila are mentioned several times (Rom 16:3-4; 1 Cor 16:19; Acts 18:2,18,26). Paul refers to two women, Euodia and Synteche, as having "labored side by side with me in the gospel" (Phil 4:2-3). His letter to the Romans acknowledges the great assistance given him by Phoebe, "a deacon of the church at Cenchreae," which was the eastern seaport of Corinth (16:1-2). Chloe was also associated with the church at Corinth (1 Cor 1:11), although we cannot determine what her role was precisely.

The church at Rome also had several women of importance in the community there. In mentioning Phoebe and Aquila (16:3), Paul asks his readers to greet "the church in their house" (16:5), which suggests that together, as owners of the house, they would have functioned as the presbyters or presidents of a eucharistic community that gathered there. Paul also mentions Mary "who has worked very hard among you" (16:6), and then Andronicus and Junia, relatives of Paul who were "prominent among the apostles [*sic*]" (16:7). He conveys greetings as well to Tryphaena and Tryphosa, whom he calls "workers in the Lord" (16:12), the mother of Rufus (16:13), Julia and the sister of Nereus (16:15), and various other "sisters" (16:14).

Q. 21. What are we to make of Paul's negative statements about women in the Church?

St. Paul's seemingly negative attitude toward women in the Church is to be found in his First Letter to the Corinthians (11:2-16 and 14:33-36). In the first passage he insists that "the husband is the head of his wife" (11:3); that women are to cover their heads while praying or prophesying (11:5); that while men are "the image and reflection of God," women are "the reflection of man" (11:7); and that the woman was created "for the sake of man" (11:9).

Exegetes point out that the Greek word for "head" in v. 3 does not connote authority or superiority, but "source." Furthermore, the Greek word for "man" in v. 7 is to be understood generically, and not in terms of the masculine gender. What is remarkable about this passage is what it takes for granted; namely, that *women* pray aloud in public liturgical assemblies and that they exercise a leadership role in the ministry of the word, that is, through prophesying (see also Acts 21:9). It is important to remember, in this connection, that prophets were among those who are reported to have presided at the Eucharist (Acts 13:1-2; also the *Didache* 10:7). Indeed, prophecy was a charism second only to the apostleship (1 Cor 12:28).

Biblical scholars regard the second passage (14:33-36) as an interpolation attributable to a source other than Paul. This is the passage in which he commands women to be silent in church, "as the law also says" (14:34). But the appeal to the law is blatantly un-Pauline and the verses directly contradict 11:5 (above) where Paul is concerned only about the head-covering of women while praying and prophesying. The injunctions, scholars argue, reflect the misogynism of 1 Tim 2:11-14 (which most scholars agree was not written by Paul) and probably stem from the same circle.

Q. 22. Among the many images of the Church, is there any one image that stands out?

No. But three images capture the mystery of the Church as well as, and perhaps much better than, any others. They are People of God, Body of Christ, and Temple of the Holy Spirit. The first highlights the Church's origin in the call of God the Father; the second underscores its sharing in the mission of Jesus Christ, the Son of God; and the third emphasizes the ongoing, intimate relationship of the Church with God the Holy Spirit.

Although the People of God image is more firmly rooted in the Old Testament, it is also clearly present in the New, especially after the early Christians began to differentiate themselves from Judaism and appropriated the designation "People of God" for themselves: "But you are a chosen race, a royal priesthood, a holy nation, God's own people, in order that you may proclaim the mighty acts of him who called you out of darkness into his marvelous light. Once you were not a people, but now you are God's people…" (1 Pet 2:9-10). The fundamental Old Testament text, "I will take you as my people, and I will be your God" (see Ezek 37:27; Exod 19:6; Isa 43:20-21; Jer 31:31-34), is cited several times throughout the New Testament and is applied to the Church (2 Cor 6:16; Heb 8:10; Titus 2:14; Rev 21:3).

Nowhere is the Church spoken of as the "new" People of God, although there is explicit mention of a "new" Covenant (Luke 22:20; 1 Cor 11:25; 2 Cor 3:6; Heb 8:13; 9:15; 12:24). A tension between the old and the new remains, especially in Romans 9–11, but the Church teaches, in the Second Vatican Council's Dogmatic Constitution on the Church, that "the people to whom the covenants and the promises were given and from whom Christ was born according to the flesh...remains most dear to God, for God does not repent of the gifts he makes nor of the calls he issues..." (n. 16).

Body of Christ is a distinctively Pauline image for the Church. It is grounded in the union between Christians and the risen Christ. Thus, when Christians share in the bread of the Eucharist, they become one body with Christ (1 Cor 10:16-17). Those who eat and drink unworthily, therefore, profane the body of Christ and are worthy of condemnation (11:27,29). It is in one body that we have been reconciled by Christ to the Father (Eph 2:16-17; Col 1:22) and it is the body of the risen Christ that we have become, in the Holy Spirit (Eph 4:4). Christ is the head of the body, which is the Church (5:23; Col 1:18; 2:19), and its principle of union and growth (Eph 4:16; Col 2:19). It is something to be built up (Eph 4:12,16). "There is one body and one Spirit..." (4:4).

Throughout much of the twentieth century and until the Second Vatican Council (1962-65), the Body of Christ image (with the modifier, "Mystical") was the dominant image for the Church. In 1943 Pope Pius XII underscored its importance in his encyclical *Mystici Corporis*. At Vatican II, however, it gave way to People of God as the dominant image.

The Church is also the Temple of the Holy Spirit. Indeed, it was traditionally understood to have been born through the outpouring of the Spirit at Pentecost (Acts 2:1-4,43-47). Thereafter, the New Testament declares, the Body of Christ "grows into a holy temple in the Lord; in whom you also are built together spiritually into a dwelling place for God" (Eph 2:21-22). Just as Jesus identified himself with the Temple, so the Church is the new Temple (1 Cor 3:9,16-17; 2 Cor 6:16; Eph 2:19-22). It is now God's dwelling place, "a reality imbued with the hidden presence of God," as the late Pope Paul VI put it in his opening address to the Second Vatican Council in 1963.

The Spirit is manifested in various ways in the Church: teaching the disciples what to say (Luke 12:12), revealing the mysteries of God (Luke 1:41,67; Acts 11:28; 13:9), inspiring prophecy (2:18), being a source of wisdom (6:3), faith (6:5; 2 Cor 4:13), encouragement (Acts 9:31), joy (13:52), hope (Rom 15:13; 1 Cor 14:14-16; 2:4-5; Gal 3:5), and love (Rom 5:5; Col 1:18; Gal 5:13-26), directing the leaders of the Church in their important decisions (Acts 13:2; 15:28; 20:28), being conferred on members at Baptism (19:2,6; 2:38-39; 15:8-9; 8:16-18; 9:17; 10:44; 11:16-17) and ordination (8:14-17; 19:6), building up the Church (1 Cor 14:12,26). Because of the Spirit's presence in the Church as in a temple, the Church is a foretaste (Rom 8:23) and a pledge (2 Cor 1:22; 5:5) of the salvation that is to come.

Q. 23. Would you say that conflicts in the Church today are worse than at any other time in history?

Not by a long shot. The Church was racked by conflict almost from the beginning. There was petty bickering even among the Apostles about who would have the highest places in the kingdom of heaven (Matt 20:20-28). The Johannine communities, as we already pointed out, were torn apart by dissension in spite of John's own emphatic message of love for one's neighbor. The earliest Jewish Christians differed sharply among themselves about how much of the Law they should continue to obey, and some of them argued bitterly with those, like Peter and Paul, who carried the Gospel to the Gentiles and then baptized them without circumcision. There were also "false teachers," against whom the Pastoral Letters railed.

Perhaps the greatest heresy during this foundational period was Gnosticism, of which the Fourth Gospel was painfully aware. Gnosticism and its cousin Docetism held that Jesus' human body was only apparent, not real. Salvation was rooted not in the humanity as well as the divinity of Jesus but in a special knowledge, or revelation, given only to the few. Marcion and his followers denied the inspired character of the Old Testament. The Montanists taught that sins committed after Baptism could not be forgiven. The Manichaeans renounced all material realities, including marriage. The Donatists insisted that a sacrament was not valid if the minister of the sacrament was in the state of mortal sin at the time he administered it.

The heresies of the fourth and fifth centuries attacked the very heart of Christian faith. Let's take Arianism as an example. Arianism denied that Jesus Christ was truly the Son of God, "of the same substance" as the Father. He was only the greatest of creatures. Even though the Church's first ecumenical council, the Council of Nicaea (325), condemned Arianism and defined the divinity of Christ, the Church lapsed into a state of pastoral confusion bordering on chaos for much of the remainder of the fourth century. The Emperor Constantine, who had called the Council of Nicaea and who was at first a supporter of its teaching, began to waver, owing perhaps to the influence of his pro-Arian sister Constantia. The leaders of the Arian party—bishops who had been exiled from their dioceses following the council—were allowed to return. At once they began to plot against their opponents. The orthodox bishop of Antioch was deposed and banished in 330 and Athanasius, the great leader of Catholic orthodoxy at Nicaea and now Bishop of Alexandria, was forced into exile in 336.

After Constantine's death in 337, Athanasius and other Nicene bishops were permitted to return to their dioceses. But the new emperor of the East, Constantius, embraced Arianism, and Athanasius was again deprived of his see in 339. In 341 a council of Eastern bishops met at Antioch and passed a series of statements with a distinctly Arian orientation. Another council met at Sardica two years later and pushed the pendulum back toward the Nicene teaching. Athanasius was restored once again as bishop of Alexandria and several Arian bishops were deposed.

But that didn't end it. Constans, the anti-Arian emperor of the Western half of the Empire, died in 350, leaving the pro-Arian Constantius as sole ruler. Successive councils were held at Sirmium (351), Arles (353), and Milan (355), at which new Arian formulations were imposed on the Western bishops. Athanasius and others were once again exiled. By 359 the situation was so confused that St. Jerome wrote his famous comment, "The whole world groaned and marvelled to find itself Arian." With the death of Constantius in 361, however, Arianism lost its chief supporter. Athanasius returned—yet again!—to his diocese of Alexandria, and the next year held a council there in which moderate Arian views were reconciled with the Nicene teaching. Athanasius died in 373, but thanks to the extraordinary theological efforts of the three Cappadocians, Basil of Caesarea, Gregory Nazianzus, and Gregory of Nyssa, Arianism was finally overcome at the Council of Constantinople in 381.

And this is only one story from the history of the Church. The next century saw the emergence of Nestorianism, which held that Jesus was actually two persons, one human and one divine, and that Mary was the mother only of the human person of Jesus, not the mother of God. Condemned by the Council of Ephesus in 431, Nestorianism was followed by Monophysitism, which held that Jesus Christ had only one nature, that his humanity was absorbed by his divinity. That, too, was condemned by the Council of Chalcedon in 451. But just mentioning the names of heresies and the councils that condemned them makes it all look too easy. Compared with the really serious and long-lasting turmoil of doctrinal controversy, depositions, exiles, and excommunications following the Council of Nicaea, for example, the post-Vatican II era with which we are immediately familiar seems utterly mild. And we haven't even mentioned the schism that has divided the Church, West from East, ever since the eleventh century, or the Protestant Reformation, which has divided the Western Church ever since the sixteenth.

Q. 24. If the universal Church is a communion of local churches, how did the local churches keep in touch with one another in the early centuries?

As some of the heresies and divisive movements spread throughout the Mediterranean world, the various Christian communities located in the major cities of the time intensified their efforts to establish contact with one another. The churches of Jerusalem, Antioch, Alexandria, Constantinople, and Seleucia in the East, and Lyons, Arles, Carthage, Trier, Barcelona, Ravenna, Milan, and Rome in the West fostered communication in various ways, such as synods or councils, the installation of bishops by neighboring bishops, the exchange of letters, the coordinating efforts of the Bishop of Rome, and even the sharing of consecrated eucharistic bread.

Synods are first mentioned in the second half of the second century. They were conducted first in Asia to combat the problem of Montanism. Differences of practice regarding the exact date for the celebration of Easter provided yet another occasion for meetings in Rome and in other centers from Gaul (modern-day France) to Mesopotamia. A controversy over Baptism prompted a synod in Carthage in 256. It is important to recall, however, that these synods were composed exclusively of bishops, but their decisions were not automatically binding on every bishop.

As the monoepiscopal form of church governance took firm hold by the end of the second century, formal liturgical rites developed for the ordination and installation of bishops. The sacramental initiation was done by the laying on of hands by bishops from neighboring churches. A local council in Arles (314) mandated that seven bishops be present, but not less than three. The practice underscored the principle that each local church, although autonomous regarding its own governance and missionary priorities, needed to be in communion with at least its neighboring Christian communities.

The exchange of letters was a time-honored way for local churches to keep in touch with one another and to foster the communion of the universal Church. Christians had been familiar with this practice from the days of St. Paul, of course. The letters were of various kinds: they conveyed absolution for sin, granted permissions, contained information about liturgical calendars and feasts, or commended the bearer to the hospitality of Christians in a distant church. Letters that were intended for an even wider circulation were the forerunner of the modern papal encyclical, which means literally a circular letter.

Another important factor—one that would increase over time to become perhaps the dominant means of inter-church communication—was the coordinating role of the Bishop of Rome. Ignatius of Antioch had already signaled its importance by conferring upon it in his letter to the Romans a "primacy of love." Even before the Council of Nicaea in 325 the church of Rome had intervened to reestablish order in troubled Corinth, became involved in a dispute about penitential practices, presumed to settle the dispute about the date of Easter, maintained a list of episcopal succession, determined appropriate liturgical practices, and undertook special collections for the support of other churches.

Finally, as a sign of their communion with other churches, Christians would send the consecrated bread of Holy Communion or fragments thereof to neighboring churches. On feast days, the bishop would send to priests or to other bishops in outlying areas a piece of newly consecrated eucharistic bread. Upon its receipt, the eucharistic bread would be mixed into a chalice as a sign of unity. The practice continued until the ninth century. There is a vestige of the practice in the celebration of the Roman liturgy today, when the consecrated host is broken and dropped into the consecrated wine just before the distribution of Holy Communion.

Communion, in every sense of the word, is what the Church is all about.

Q. 25. I've read somewhere that the so-called "Barbarian Invasions" had a lot to do with the way the Church developed in the Middle Ages and even today. What impact, if any, did they have on the life of the Church?

Referring to this phenomenon as "so-called" is good for starters. Many of us probably have mental images of hordes of bearded men, half-draped in lion skins, brandishing heavy maces, looting and pillaging everything in sight. Some of this was surely true, but it is largely a product of exaggeration. For the most part the "Barbarian Invasions" were really the migrations of various pagan tribal groups (Germans, Saracens, Scandinavians, and Vikings) looking for a better place to settle down and live a more peaceful and prosperous life together. The migrations began at the beginning of the fifth century and lasted some 600 years.

Those who converted to Christianity after coming into contact with Christians did so tribally, not individually. Such was the case, for example, of the Frankish tribes under Clovis (d. 511). Because the decision to enter the Church was made at the top, the rank-and-file had, at best, only a superficial understanding of the doctrinal and moral content of their new religion. Not surprisingly, superstitious practices and vestiges of pagan worship remained for many centuries. Many of those who became Christian after entering the Roman Empire turned to Arianism.

The strongly militaristic and feudal elements in Germanic culture influenced Germanic Christian devotion, spirituality, and ecclesiastical organization. Christ was regarded as the *Heiland*, the most powerful of kings. The place of worship was called the *Burg-Gottes*, God's fortress. Monks were depicted as the warriors of Christ. The profession of faith was equivalent to an oath of fidelity to one's feudal lord. The insignia of office (crosier, ring, miter) were a carry-over from those of the tribal chieftains. The settling of legal disputes by physical combat, rather than by due process, encouraged the alternative Christian practice of compensation, whereby money was given to make satisfaction for crimes—the forerunner of the medieval system of indulgences.

Unlike the ancient Christian-Roman law, German law held to a more political idea of church office. Therefore, it was less concerned with the moral and pastoral qualifications of a bishop or an abbot than with his administrative abilities and his loyalty to the ones who appointed him. The feudal system of vassals and lords, now applied to the Church, prepared the way for the investiture controversy in the eleventh century between the popes (and especially Gregory VII) and the rulers of the state. The argument was over the power of appointment of bishops and abbots and the right to invest them with the insignia of office. It was the papacy's vigorous response to the challenge of lay encroachment into the internal life of the Church that accounts in large part for the sudden inflation of papal authority that occurred at the beginning of the second Christian millennium and that has endured ever since.

Q. 26. There have been over 260 popes in the history of the Church. Why do you say that Gregory VII was one of the most important?

One of the greatest theologians of the twentieth century, the Dominican Yves Congar, whom Pope John Paul II created a cardinal in 1994, at age 90, has said that there is "no doubt" in his mind that "the great turning point" in ecclesiology (that aspect of theology that focuses on the nature and mission of the Church) is the eleventh century, and that the turning point is "embedded in the person" of Pope Gregory VII (see *Fifty Years of Catholic Theology: Conversations with Yves Congar*, ed. Bernard Lauret, Philadelphia: Westminster Press, 1988, pp. 40-44).

Because of his severe problems with lay rulers, Gregory asked his canon lawyers to locate and bring together the greatest possible number of texts on papal power. This research culminated, after the death of Gregory, in the famous Decree of Gratian in 1140. The Decree gave the Church an enormous and often contradictory collection of documents drawn from councils, popes, and the Fathers of the Church. Unfortunately, the texts were arbitrarily mixed together, without distinction, under the same headings and in the same chapters. That paved the way for their being used simply to bolster a particular argument without regard for historical accuracy or context.

This new and concentrated appeal to law, under pressure of lay encroachments, propelled the papacy and the Catholic Church onto a legalistic course from which we have not substantially veered ever since. Thus, in opposing the temporal powers, Cardinal Congar has pointed out, the Church was led to adopt very much the same attitudes as the temporal powers themselves, that is, to conceive of itself as a juridical society and as an institutional power, when in reality it is a communion of grace, a mystery, with ministers who are pastoral servants, not juridical authorities. Another reason why the Church became a legal institution, Congar continued, was "the affirmation of papal power as the basis of everything." In Gregory's own famous *Dictatus Papae* (1075), containing twenty-seven "incredible" propositions (to use Congar's adjective), it is asserted that a simple papal delegate, a nuncio, even if he is not a bishop (many, in fact, were deacons), has authority over bishops, archbishops, and all the rest of the Church. "That shows," Cardinal Congar observed, "how the legal has priority over the sacramental."

An unhappy effect of this development toward legalism became evident toward the middle of the twelfth century when the term "Body of Christ," whose original application was to the Eucharist and to the Church as a eucharistic community, came to be applied to the Church as a juridical and hierarchical society. "In the end," Congar insisted, "the Church is certainly a society, but that is not what one should begin with. The first thing is a spiritual communion, a communion on the basis of the Word of God received in faith and grace, of which the sacraments are one of the principal vehicles."

None of this should lead one to neglect, however, the serious reforms that Gregory VII did successfully introduce into the Church at this time. He cracked down on the buying and selling of ecclesiastical offices and spiritual goods (known as simony), on the passing of church property into the private hands of a bishop's or a priest's off-spring or relatives (known as the alienation of property), and, of course, on the interference of lay rulers in the internal life of the Church (known as lay investiture). Unfortunately, the Gregorian Reform had other, unintended results.

Q. 27. How has canon law affected the life and practice of the Church?

Perhaps the principal unintended result of the Gregorian Reform was the dominance of canon law in the Catholic Church during its entire second millennium of existence. Gratian's collection and sys-tematization of ecclesiastical laws, which appeared in 1150 under the title, *The Concord of Discordant Canons*, became the basic text of a whole new branch of theological studies, called canon law. Legal degrees rather than the Gospel became the immediate and primary basis for moral judgments. Indeed, a knowledge of canon law became the requisite for ecclesiastical advancement, and it remained so until the post-Vatican II period.

Even the sacraments were affected—so much so, in fact, that a kind of sacramental jurisprudence developed. The primary questions posed about the sacraments were not, for example, How does a sacra-ment initiate us into the mysteries of God? but Who can administer a sacrament? Who is eligible to receive a sacrament? When and under what circumstances can one receive a sacrament? Baptism was por-trayed not as a rebirth in Christ and the beginning of one's initiation into the mystery of the Church, along with Confirmation and Eucharist, but as a juridical act by which one becomes a member of an organized society, with full rights, privileges, and obligations. Matrimony was considered less a celebration and ratification of a cou-ple's mutual love and their promise of mutual fidelity, than a legal con-tract whose validity depended upon the absence of any one of a long list of impediments drawn up by Rome.

But perhaps the principal effect of this canonical turn was the inordinate inflation of papal powers and prerogatives. By 1234 all pre-vious collections of papal decisions were combined and codified by

Pope Gregory IX (1227-41) into *The Five Books of Decretals*. The juridical doctrine of the Church was now clearly and firmly established. The Church was understood as a visible, hierarchically structured society with supreme power vested in the pope, who stood, as it were, atop a pyramid, with the cardinals, archbishops, bishops, clergy, religious, and laity below him in a descending order of authority. Many rights formerly exercised by bishops and synods were now reserved to the pope. Even the election of the pope was placed in the hands of cardinals who were themselves directly appointed by the pope. Bishops were now required to swear an oath of obedience to the pope—oaths that closely resembled feudal oaths that bound a vassal to his lord.

The pope was no longer consecrated. Instead, he was crowned with a tiara, a helmet-shaped head covering used originally by the deified rulers of Persia. The papal coronation rite was more like that of an emperor than of the "servant of the servants of God." Not until 1978—after Vatican II and the decline of the canonical model of the Church—did the practice of coronation end. Pope John Paul I chose instead to be "installed" into his new "supreme pastoral ministry." When Pope John Paul II succeeded John Paul I the following month, he, too, refused to be crowned in imperial style.

Q. 28. We have always heard a lot about "bad popes," but other than the infamous Alexander VI, how many "bad popes" have there been, and what difference do they make to Catholic belief in the pope?

It is impossible to count the "good" popes and the "bad" popes. Some popes were wonderfully spiritual men who failed in their efforts to advance the mission of the Church. Were they "good" popes or "bad" ones? Other popes were extraordinarily successful in protecting the spiritual and temporal interests of the Church, even in reforming it, but also led less than exemplary personal lives. On which list would they belong? But surely no one can quarrel with your reference to Alexander VI. He started early on the path to corruption. As vice-chancellor of the Holy See he had amassed such wealth that he was considered the second richest cardinal in the Church. At the same time, he lived an openly licentious life, fathering several children. He was elected to the papacy in 1492, the year Columbus discovered America, by bribing several of the cardinal-electors and promising others rich preferments. Once in office he continued his quest of gold and women, but also dedicated himself to the enrichment and advancement of his relatives. For example, he named his 18-year-old son Caesare bishop of several dioceses and then a cardinal. Alexander's death in 1503 was officially attributed to malaria, but some historians believe that he and his son Caesare were victims of a poison that had been intended for a cardinal who was their host at dinner but was mistakenly given to them.

Perhaps the worst string of so-called "bad popes" came in the tenth century, when the papacy was, for all practical purposes, the plaything of various powerful Roman families. Among the most corrupt was Pope John XII (955-64), who was only 18 when elected. According to contemporary reports, he had no interest in spiritual matters, was addicted to "boorish pleasures," and led such an "unhibitedly debauched life" that some accused him of turning the Lateran palace into a brothel. How did he ever get elected? He was the illegitimate son of Alberic II, the ruling prince of Rome, who on his deathbed made the leading Romans swear that they would elect his son pope upon the death of the incumbent, Agapitus II. John himself died of a stroke at age 27, allegedly while in bed with a married woman.

Corrupt popes do not undermine the validity of the papacy any more than sinful Christians undermine the validity of the Church, which is, after all, divine as well as human. Popes, on the other hand, are *only* human. Saying this doesn't justify the existence of "bad popes," like Alexander VI or John XII. It only makes the point that official Catholic teaching about the papacy does not depend upon the goodness or even the saintliness of individual popes. Even Peter himself denied Jesus after he was taken away to be tried before Pilate and crucified. The Church of modern times has been particularly fortunate, however, in the spiritual quality of the men whom it has elevated to the papal office. Even when there have been strong differences of opinion within the Church about papal policies, none of the popes of the past two centuries bear the slightest resemblance to Alexander VI or to some of the notorious characters who occupied the seat of Peter during the tenth century.

Q. 29. Who were the antipopes?

An antipope was an individual whose claim to the papacy has been rejected by the Church as invalid. Unfortunately, it has not always been easy for the Church to make that judgment because the rules for papal elections have changed over time, and in some cases these rules have been bypassed. We have already pointed out that the dying Alberic II, prince ruler of Rome, made the papal electors swear that they would elect his son pope once the office became vacant. (They did, and the new pope was John XII.) This was in direct violation of the decree of Pope Symmachus (499) forbidding such agreements about papal succession while the reigning pope was still alive. Innocent II (1130-43), for example, was elected by a minority of cardinals in a clandestine meeting, in another flagrant violation of the rules, but he is still considered a valid pope. Nor is personal sanctity a reliable determinant of popes versus antipopes. The man considered to be the first antipope, Hippolytus (217–ca.235), was a martyr and a saint, while a canonically legitimate pope like John XII (955-64) was excommunicated and deposed by a Roman synod for gross immorality.

The most famous antipopes were Benedict XIII and John XXIII (not to be confused with the validly elected John XXIII of modern times), who were among the claimants to the papal throne alongside Gregory XII, the one the Church has subsequently recognized as valid, during the Great Western Schism (1378-1417). But the Schism itself did not end until the antipopes Benedict XIII and John XXIII were formally deposed by the Council of Constance (1414–18), Gregory XII voluntarily abdicated, and Martin V was elected. Ironically, Martin V (as Cardinal Oddo Colonna) had broken earlier with Gregory XII, was active in preparing the Council of Pisa (1409) that deposed Gregory, and was a supporter of the antipope John XXIII until John's flight from Rome in disguise. John XXIII accepted his own deposition by the Council of Constance, but Benedict XIII and his successor, Clement VIII, held out for another ten years or so, but with only tiny followings.

The thirty-ninth and last of the antipopes was Felix V (1439-49). He had been elected by the rump Council of Basel after it had deposed Martin V's legitimate successor, Eugene IV. Felix's election was irregular in every sense, having been carried out by only one cardinal and thirty-two electors nominated by a commission. His election was not widely recognized, but he named several eminent men as cardinals (some declined) and for a time employed a future pope, Enea Silvio Piccolomini (later Pius II) as his secretary. When Nicholas V succeeded Eugene IV in 1447, Felix abdicated and retracted all the censures he had leveled at his adversaries. In return Nicholas V appointed him cardinal-bishop of Santa Sabina, with a handsome pension, and also papal vicar and legate in Savoy and adjacent dioceses. Such are the vicissitudes and ironies of papal history.

Q. 30. I take it that the history of the popes contains a lot of unusual stories. Is there any one that stands out from the rest?

My personal favorite is the story of Pope Formosus (891-96) because it so directly contradicts the naively romantic ideas so many Catholics still have about the papacy.

Formosus was a gifted and well educated man who had a brilliant missionary career in Bulgaria and as a papal legate in France and Germany. As bishop of the diocese of Porto in Italy, he served as a consecrator of Pope Stephen V in 885. Although already over the age of 75, he was elected Stephen's successor six years later. But in order to become the new bishop of Rome, he had to leave his diocese of Porto. The idea of a bishop's transferring from a smaller diocese to another, larger one was not yet customary, as it is today, and that fact would later be used against Formosus in a heretofore unimagined way.

Formosus died after only four and a half years in office, but his troubles were only beginning. Nine months later his decaying corpse was exhumed, propped up on a throne in full pontifical vestments, and then solemnly arraigned in a mock trial (known in history as the "cadaver synod"), presided over by none other than Pope Stephen VI. A deacon stood by Formosus' corpse, answering the charges on the dead pope's behalf.

Formosus was found guilty of perjury, of having coveted the papal throne, and of having violated the canons of the Church that forbade the transfer of bishops from one diocese to another. All of his official acts and ordinations as pope were declared null and void. The three fingers of his right hand which he had used to swear and to bless were hacked off, and his body was reburied in a common grave. The body was then dig up a second time and flung into the Tiber River. A hermit found the corpse and reburied it.

A more sympathetic successor in the papacy, Pope Theodore II, ordered Formosus' body dug up a third time, had it reclothed in pontifical vestments, and then reburied—a fourth time—in its original grave in St. Peter's. He also nullified Pope Stephen VI's order and declared that all of Formosus' ordinations had been valid. But another successor, Pope Sergius III, reversed Pope Theodore's action and declared once again that all of Formosus' ordinations had been invalid. The Church was thrown into total confusion because Pope Formosus had ordained many bishops and they, in turn, had ordained many more priests, some of whom later became bishops themselves and ordained many more priests, and so on.

If history is, as Pope John XXIII (1958-63) was fond of saying, "the great teacher of life," we should have something to learn from the story of Pope Formosus and the grotesque way he was treated by two later popes. If it is always the case that the successor of Peter guarantees a sure path to unity and truth, what is to be said of this situation? After all, Popes Stephen VI and Sergius III were as much "successors of Peter" as the present pope is.

Is anyone surprised, by the way, that we have never had a Pope Formosus II?

Q. 31. Why did the Greek and Russian Orthodox break away from the Catholic Church?

A complete answer to this question would be long and complicated. I'll try to be brief. What you're really asking about is the origin of the East-West Schism, or the breach in unity between the Latin churches of the West, under the lead of the Bishop of Rome, and the Greek churches of the East, under the lead of the Patriarch of Constantinople. But this breach did not occur at any one point in time. It was the result of a gradual and painful process of misunderstanding and bad behavior.

From the time of the Council of Chalcedon in 451 when Rome rejected the proposal to grant major jurisdictional powers to

Constantinople, relations between Rome (representing the Western, or Latin, Church) and Constantinople (representing the Eastern, or Greek, Church) have been marked by sporadic tension, conflict, and eventual schism, or the formal breaking of communion between churches. The gap was widened further in the eighth century when the Eastern emperors tried to enforce a policy of iconoclasm (the abolition of religious images). By this time the West could no longer understand Greek and so it could not appreciate the distinction between "veneration" and "adoration." Where the Easterners recommended the former, the Westerners thought they meant the latter.

The next major breach occurred in 858 when the emperor deposed the patriarch of Constantinople and replaced him with Photius, against Pope Nicholas I's wishes. The pope sent legates to Constantinople who decided in favor of Photius, but Photius himself balked, insisting that he did not accept the supremacy of the pope. The pope withdrew his support. Peace was restored at a council held in Constantinople in 879, but it came apart definitively almost two centuries later when another misunderstanding developed, this time between Cerularius, patriarch of Constantinople, and Pope Leo IX regarding the liturgical use of Latin in the East and Greek in the West. When legates from Rome arrived in Constantinople in 1054, they marched into the Church of Santa Sophia just before the afternoon liturgy and laid on the altar a bull excommunicating Cerularius, the emperor, and all their supporters. Then they ostentatiously shook the dust from their feet and marched out.

There were other efforts at reconciliation thereafter, especially with the election of Pope Urban II in 1088, and later still with two ecumenical councils (Lyons [1276] and Florence [1439]), but none succeeded for more than a time. The *coup de grace* was probably dealt during the Fourth Crusade (1202-1204) when Western knights sacked the city of Constantinople, including the churches, in 1203, and drove out the Greek patriarch and replaced him with a Latin patriarch. The climate did not really begin to improve again until December 7, 1965, the day before the Second Vatican Council adjourned, when Pope Paul VI and the ecumenical patriarch Athenagoras mutually lifted the anathemas of 1054.

Q. 32. Wasn't there a situation back in the Middle Ages when three cardinals claimed to be pope, all at the same time? How did this come about, and how was the problem resolved?

I have already referred to the Great Western Schism in an earlier answer about the antipopes (Q. 26). The papacy returned to Rome in 1378 after almost seventy years of "Babylonian Captivity" in Avignon, France. In April of that year the College of Cardinals, under immense pressure from the Roman citizenry, elected an Italian, the archbishop of Bari, who took the name Urban VI. Almost immediately, however, the new pope displayed an intransigent personality and a violent temper. Many thought him deranged. The French cardinals withdrew to Anagni where they eventually decided that Urban's election had been null and void because it was carried out under undue pressure. They proclaimed a new pope, Cardinal Robert of Geneva, who took the name Clement VII. Now the Church had two claimants to the see of Peter and a schism was on.

In 1409 at a council held in Pisa a third pope was elected, Alexander V. Meanwhile, Benedict XIII had succeeded Clement VII, and Gregory XII was in office as the fourth pope in the so-called "Roman line" during the Schism (Urban VI, the pope elected after the papacy's return from Avignon, was, in turn, succeeded by Boniface IX and Innocent VII). By the end of his reign, Benedict had no support outside the small Spanish town where he lived, and Gregory—the valid pope—had the allegiance only of certain Italian princes. Ironically, the one who had the least claim to the papacy, Alexander V, actually enjoyed the widest support. Upon Alexander's death, the Council of Pisa elected John XXIII, who proceeded to alienate most of his original supporters. The emperor forced John to call a new council—which he did, at Constance in 1414. More than 100,000 descended upon the city. Theologians and canonists voted alongside the bishops at the council.

When John saw the handwriting on the wall, he fled the city, was caught and arrested, then placed under guard. He was formally deposed after a trial. Gregory XII, now 89 years of age and refusing to leave Rimini to attend the council, sent representatives to Constance who formally convoked the council. He then abdicated. The third claimant to the papacy, Benedict XIII, was also condemned, but he refused to resign. On St. Martin's day, November 11, 1417, the conclave of twen-

ty-three cardinals and five prelates from each of the five nations represented at the council elected a new pope who took the name Martin V.
The Great Western Schism was over.

Q. 33. You mentioned conciliarism in reference to the Great Western Schism. What is conciliarism?

In the face of the terrible threat to the unity of the Church posed
by the Great Western Schism, key members of the Church turned to a
theory known as conciliarism, originally developed by canonists in the
twelfth century. According to conciliarism, ecclesiastical power resides
ultimately in the whole body of the faithful, not in its leaders. The
leaders possess and exercise this power only because it has been transferred to them by the faithful, as in the case of the College of Cardinals
when it elects a new pope. For the conciliarist, there are, in effect, two
churches: the universal Church (all the faithful) and the Apostolic
Church (the administrative arm of the universal Church). The latter is
always subordinate to the former. The only true representative of the
universal Church is a general, or ecumenical, council. The pope himself is subject to such a council.

Conciliarism received a decided boost from the Council of
Constance which successfully resolved the Great Western Schism. In
1415 the council passed a decree entitled *Haec Sancta*, which espoused
the supremacy of a general council and the collegiality of the bishops.
In 1417 the decree *Frequens* was enacted, mandating that there be a
general council after five, seven, and then every ten years, each one
announced by the previous one.

Although the new pope, Martin V, generally approved the
decrees and did call a council at Pavia five years later, it was evident
that he and his immediate successors were not enthusiastic about conciliarism. Indeed, Eugene IV suspended the next general council at
Basel and transferred it to Florence in 1431. It was at Basel that conciliarism reached its high-point. In 1460, however, Pope Pius II (who,
ironically, had once served as secretary to an antipope) issued a decree
condemning the "deadly poison" of conciliarism and condemning
under pain of excommunication any appeal beyond a pope to a general
council. That prohibition was repeated by Sixtus IV and Julius II.

Among the strongest opponents of the pope's negative stance

toward general councils were members of the reformed monastic groups, especially the Carthusians. They argued that the pope's resistance to the conciliar principle was rooted in the Roman Curia's fear of being held accountable for centuries of evil practices. This was not the first, nor would it be the last, attack upon the Roman Curia. But even with the support of the Carthusians, conciliarism died on the vine.

Q. 34. In this age of ecumenism, has the thinking of the Catholic Church changed regarding the Protestant Reformation?

Generally, yes. In fact, the Second Vatican Council's Decree on Ecumenism explicitly acknowledges that "both sides were to blame" for the rupture of unity in the sixteenth century. The council also emphasized that "one cannot impute the sin of separation to those who at present are born into these [non-Catholic churches] and are instilled therein with Christ's faith. The Catholic Church accepts them with respect and affection as brothers and sisters" (n. 3).

At one time, Catholics were told that the Reformation only happened because Martin Luther wanted to break his vow of celibacy to marry a nun. We know now that it's a little more complicated than that. First of all, the Reformation is really a series of reformations. There was the so-called Magisterial Reformation of Martin Luther and Jean Calvin. Then there was the English Reformation under King Henry VIII, which produced the Church of England and eventually the Anglican Communion of churches. Finally, there was the Radical Reformation of the Anabaptists, Mennonites, and others who regarded the mainline Reformers as still too Catholic.

The causes of the Reformation go far beyond Luther's desire to marry or Henry VIII's desire to divorce his first wife and marry a second. There were at least six major causes of the Protestant Reformation: (1) the corruption of the papacy during the Renaissance years when nepotism, simony, military expeditions, financial manipulations, and political intrigues marked too many pontificates; (2) the divorce of piety from theology, and of theology from the Bible, which left the masses vulnerable to the "alluring simplicity" of the Reformers' message; (3) the debilitating after-effects of the Western Schism, especially on the credibility and effectiveness of the papacy; (4) the rise of the national state and the growth of nationalism; (5) the close connection between Western Christianity and Western civilization, such that the leadership of the Church, especially the papacy, assumed an imperial cast; and (6) the strong personalities—with their peculiar strengths and weaknesses—of Luther, Calvin, and Ulrich Zwingli.

After centuries of animosity and sterile opposition, Catholics have come to accept Protestants, Anglicans, and separated Eastern Christians as fellow members of the Body of Christ—people who "believe in Christ and have been properly baptized" and who are thereby "brought into a certain, though imperfect, communion with the Catholic Church." Whatever differences exist between us are differences of "degrees." However, in spite of those differences, we are all "justified by faith through baptism" and as such are "incorporated into Christ." Therefore, non-Catholic Christians "have a right to be honored by the title of Christian, and are properly regarded as brothers and sisters in the Lord by...the Catholic Church" (n. 3).

Q. 35. How did the Catholic Church respond to the Reformation?

Not very well at first. In spite of the fact that Luther himself had called for a general council to examine his doctrine, nothing was done until 1545 with the calling of the Council of Trent. However, by the 1530s all of Scandinavia, the British Isles, and much of Germany, Austria, and France had severed the bonds of unity with Rome. With the smell of conciliarism still in the air, the pope was fearful of calling a council that might abolish the papacy. He was also caught, as a temporal ruler, between the territorial designs of the Hapsburgs, on the one hand, and the king of France, on the other.

Not until the election of Paul III in 1534 did the seriousness of the situation begin to be recognized. He called for a reform of the Roman Curia, particularly in financial matters. The centerpiece of his reform was the Council of Trent, which began small (less than forty bishops, mostly Italian, attended the opening) but by the time it ended in 1563 it had established itself as the most important doctrinal and disciplinary council in history. It is fair to say that from this time until the Second Vatican Council in 1962, Catholicism was thoroughly dominated by the letter and spirit of Trent.

Doctrinally, the council marked a course between Pelagianism (everything depends on human effort) and Protestantism (everything depends on God), insisting that salvation comes from God as a pure gift, but that it requires some measure of human cooperation. The council also clearly defined the meaning and number of the seven sacraments, especially the Eucharist, and decreed that marriages had to be celebrated before a priest and two witnesses and that marriages between Catholics and Protestants were invalid. The council created the Index of Forbidden Books and established seminaries for the training and spiritual formation of priests.

At the heart of the Catholic Counter-Reformation was the newly established Society of Jesus, known simply as the Jesuits. Although only one of many new religious communities in the Church, the Jesuits stood out because of their dedication to key aspects of the apostolate, including especially education of the young and future priests and missionary work. They had more than 13,000 members within fifty years of St. Ignatius of Loyola's death in 1556.

Unfortunately, the post-Tridentine Church tended to be more reactive than proactive. It continued to emphasize those doctrines and practices that the Protestants attacked: veneration of the saints, Marian devotions, eucharistic adoration, the Mass as a sacrifice performed only by the ordained priest. Not until Vatican II did this reactive phase come to an end.

Q. 36. Most of us are at least generally aware of the Second Vatican Council and of its overall importance in the life of the Church today, but we don't hear very much, if anything at all, concerning the First Vatican Council. What was that council all about, and does it continue to have any significance for Catholics today?

The First Vatican Council, the largest general council of the Church to that point in history (1869-70), issued only two documents: a dogmatic constitution on faith and a dogmatic constitution on the Church. The document on faith rejected two extreme views circulating in the nineteenth century: Rationalism on the left and Fideism on the right. Rationalism held that reason alone is the final arbiter of truth. Fideism held that reason plays no part at all in our coming to faith or in our understanding of faith. The council struck a middle course. Our faith is "consonant with reason," and our reason is "illumined by faith." Faith and reason are partners, not adversaries. They work together just as grace and nature do in the human person, and divinity and humanity do in the person of Jesus Christ. It's not a matter of faith alone or reason alone, but of both together.

The second document of the First Vatican Council was its constitution on the Church. The two principal teachings of this document concerned papal primacy and papal infallibility. The council solemnly taught that the pope, as Bishop of Rome, is the earthly head of the Church. He is not simply "first among equals," as the Anglican Communion views the Archbishop of Canterbury, for example. Moreover, the pope's authoritative teachings are not subject to the juridical consent of the entire Church, embodied in a formal vote taken by a general council or other representative agency in the Church. This was the position taken at the time by those identified with Gallicanism, a movement centered especially in France (ancient Gaul). The council also solemnly declared that when the pope teaches in his capacity as earthly head of the Church, that is, *ex cathedra*, "from the chair" of authority, on some matter pertaining to faith or morals, with the clear intention of binding the whole Church, that teaching is infallible (literally, immune from error).

Although the teaching of the First Vatican Council on faith and the papacy remains an essential part of the Church's official teaching, the Second Vatican Council deepened and enriched that teaching. In its Dogmatic Constitution on Divine Revelation the council taught that faith is an act of personal trust and obedience and not simply the intellectual acceptance of a body of truths (n. 5), and in its Dogmatic Constitution on the Church the council taught that the pastoral role and authority of the pope are never separate from the whole college of bishops, of which the pope is the presiding member (n. 22). The Second Vatican Council also reiterated and reinforced the teaching of the First Vatican Council that the infallibility which the pope exercises is the infallibility of the whole Church and not of himself alone (n. 25).

Q. 37. I've heard some Catholics complain that there is a new wave of Modernism in the Church today. What's wrong with being "modern"? Isn't it better to be up-to-date than behind-the-times?

Modernism doesn't mean being "modern" in the sense in which you've taken it. It refers rather to a complex of movements in the Catholic Church of the late nineteenth and early twentieth centuries. Some aspects of Modernism would be, by present theological and doctrinal standards, entirely orthodox. Others would not.

In its unorthodox forms Modernism tended to downplay doctrine and the supernatural order generally, in favor of inner religious experience and historico-critical thought, for example, looking upon the Bible as a purely historical document, to be studied without any doctrinal presuppositions.

Modernism, however, was ahead of its time in other respects. The inner religious experience *is* an essential element of the life of faith and spirituality. Authentic Christianity cannot be measured by adherence to doctrine and church discipline alone. Second, dogmatic and other doctrinal formulations are always inadequate to the reality they attempt to capture. Ultimately, that reality is God, and God is ever elusive, always ineffable. Third, revelation is not primarily to satisfy our intellectual curiosity about divine and supernatural realities, but rather for salvation and the quality of human life here on earth in anticipation of our eternal life in heaven. Fourth, revelation did not come to us ready-made, in final form. It is only gradually unfolded in history and in the life of the Church. Fifth, the Bible is the word of God in human words, which means that, although it is inspired, it can and must be read, studied, and interpreted according to the most scientifically critical methods at hand.

It is difficult for us today to imagine how highly charged the atmosphere in the Church was during the anti-Modernist years. It seemed that practically every scholar, every teacher of theology, and even a future pope like John XXIII was under suspicion. There even existed an officially created spy network to detect heresy or other forms of dissident thinking and teaching and to receive complaints from all around the world. In 1907 the Holy Office (now the Congregation for the Doctrine of Faith) issued a condemnatory decree, *Lamentabili*, and Pope Pius X published an encyclical highly critical of

what it took to be Modernism, *Pascendi*. Two years later an Oath
Against Modernism was imposed on all clergy, including those about
to be ordained, given a pastorate, made a bishop, or beginning a teaching career in a seminary.

Unfortunately, then as now the word "Modernism" was thrown
around quite carelessly so that it applied to just about any debatable
position that differed from the strictest conservative viewpoint. When
Catholics hurl the charge of "Modernism" today, it is usually against
those who are simply trying their best to articulate the faith in a manner consistent with developments in Catholic biblical scholarship over
the past fifty years and the teachings of the Second Vatican Council
itself.

Q. 38. What is an ecumenical council, and how does its authority differ from the pope's?

An ecumenical council is an assembly that represents the whole
Church. The Greek word, *oikoumene*, from which the English word
"ecumenical" is derived, means "the whole, wide world." Ecumenical
councils, therefore, are distinguished from world synods of bishops (of
which there have been several since the Second Vatican Council), ple-
nary councils (such as the three councils of Baltimore in the nineteenth
century), provincial councils (involving several adjoining dioceses),
regional councils (involving more than one province), and diocesan
councils, or synods. An ecumenical council is the highest doctrinal and
disciplinary authority in the Church.

If an ecumenical council is the highest doctrinal and disciplinary
authority in the Church, where does that leave the pope? The pope also
is the highest doctrinal and disciplinary authority in the Church. Does
that mean we have two supreme authorities? If so, isn't that a contradiction in terms? It may appear to be the case, but it isn't.

An ecumenical council's authority isn't set in opposition to the
pope's because an ecumenical council always includes the pope, as its
head, or presiding bishop. An ecumenical council never acts without
the pope. On the other hand, whenever the pope acts in his capacity as
the head of the college of bishops, he does not act independently of
that college. He acts always in union with the bishops, not apart from

them. For example, in his 1995 encyclical *Evangelium Vitae* ("The Gospel of Life"), Pope John Paul II adopted a teaching formula on three different issues—direct and voluntary killing of the innocent, abortion, and euthanasia—that clearly situated his own teaching authority in the context of the teaching authority of all of his brother bishops: "by the authority which Christ conferred upon Peter and his successors, in communion with the bishops...."

There have been twenty-one ecumenical councils in the history of the Church. The first was at Nicaea in 325 and the most recent was the Second Vatican Council (1962-65). Among the most important councils were Constantinople (381), Ephesus (431), Chalcedon (451), Lateran IV (1215), Constance (1414-18), Trent (1545-63), and Vatican I (1869-70). According to canon law, ecumenical councils have to be called by the pope, but that wasn't always the case. The first eight councils were called by the emperor and were held in the East. The pope didn't personally attend, but gave his subsequent approval. For those of us familiar only with the Second Vatican Council, these facts are not easy to assimilate and digest.

Q. 39. You say that there have been twenty-one ecumenical councils in the history of the Church and that some are more important than others. Where do you place the Second Vatican Council?

Future historians will be in a far better position to judge the relative importance of ecumenical councils than we can today, but surely the Second Vatican Council is bound to stand out as one of the most important of all time, and certainly the most significant religious event since the Protestant Reformation of the sixteenth century.

In terms of total number of delegates, or "fathers," Vatican II was larger than any of the preceding twenty councils. The largest previous ecumenical council had been Vatican I (1869-70), with 737 in attendance. Vatican II had more than 2600 bishops from all over the globe. While Vatican I was dominated by Europeans, Vatican II included every national and ethnic group from around the world. This was due to the Church's extraordinary success between Vatican I and Vatican II in building native clergies and hierarchies. Among eligible bishops at

Vatican II, 1089 were from Europe, 489 from South America, 404 from North America, 374 from Asia, 296 from Africa, 84 from Central America, and 75 from Oceania.

The council was also more ecumenical than previous councils. There were some 40 non-Catholic observers at the first session (1962), but none from the Orthodox churches. By the beginning of the second session (1963), there were 63 observers from almost every major Christian church, including three from the Russian Orthodox Church. By the end of the council (1965), there were 80 observers in all. Eleven laymen were invited to attend the second session, but by the beginning of the fourth and final session there were 52 lay auditors, 29 of whom were men and 23 women, including 10 nuns.

But sheer numbers, broad ecumenical participation, and the presence of nuns, laymen, and laywomen do not in themselves make Vatican II an important council. The Council of Constance in the fifteenth century, for example, had an extraordinary number of laity, religious, and so-called lower clergy as active participants and even as voting members. Vatican II was unique in the history of the Church because it was the first council to have been called, not to combat heresy or to deal with a crisis in the Church, but to bring the Church up to date (Italian, *aggiornamento*) so that it could preach the Gospel to the modern world more effectively. The council's purpose, as stated in Pope John XXIII's opening address, was not to repeat traditional doctrinal formulations or to condemn error but to eradicate the seeds of discord and to promote the peace and unity of all humanity.

Again, future historians will have to judge, but from our own limited vantage point it seems that Vatican II brought the Church to the threshold of the third Christian millennium in which the Church would become, for the first time, a truly world Church, multicultural and catholic in the fullest sense of the words.

Q. 40. You said earlier that the First Vatican Council was important for its teaching on faith and on the papacy. What was the Second Vatican Council's most important teaching?

The Second Vatican Council's primary focus was on the Church itself, and its teachings covered a fairly wide theological and pastoral territory. The council taught, first, that the Church is a mystery, or sacrament, and not primarily an organization or institution. Second, that the Church is the whole People of God, and not just the hierarchy, the clergy, or the religiously professed. Third, that the Church's mission is for the sake of the Reign of God and that the Church itself is always subordinate to the Reign of God. Fourth, that the Church's mission includes the social apostolate (action on behalf of justice, ministry to those in need) and is not limited to preaching, teaching, and the celebration of the sacraments. Fifth, that the Church is a communion, or college, of local churches, which are not simply portions of the universal Church. They are the Body of Christ in their own particular place. Sixth, that the Church is a pilgrim community, which means that it is still on the way toward the final Reign of God and is always in need of penance and renewal. Seventh, that the laity participate directly in the mission of the Church and are not simply sharers in the mission of the hierarchy. Eighth, that all authority in the Church is to be exercised as a service and in a collegial and collaborative manner. Ninth, that the Body of Christ includes all Christian churches and is not limited exclusively to the Catholic Church, and certainly not to the Roman Catholic Church. Tenth, that God uses not only other Christian churches but also non-Christian religions in offering salvation to all humankind, and that the Catholic Church, therefore, is not the only means of salvation.

These teachings on the Church are to be found, in one form or another, in the sixteen documents of the Second Vatican Council. Each of them is concerned, in varying degrees, with the mystery and mission of the Church. The council's principal teachings on the Church are presented in the Dogmatic Constitution on the Church (*Lumen Gentium*) and the Pastoral Constitution on the Church in the Modern World (*Gaudium et Spes*). The former emphasizes the inner life of the Church and the latter, the Church's relationship to the world. The Decree on Ecumenism (*Unitatis Redintegratio*), the Declaration on the Relationship between the Church and Non-Christian Religions (*Nostra Aetate*), and the Declaration on Religious Freedom (*Dignitatis Humanae*) are concerned with the Catholic Church's relationship with non-Catholic Christian and non-Christian religious communities as well as the body politic. The Decree on the Church's Missionary Activity (*Ad Gentes*) stresses teachings already present in *Lumen Gentium* and *Gaudium et Spes*. The Decree on Eastern Catholic Churches (*Orientalium Ecclesiarum*) reminds Roman Catholics that there is a Catholic communion of churches that includes more than the Roman Church. The Constitution on the Sacred Liturgy (*Sacrosanctum Concilium*), the Dogmatic Constitution on Divine Revelation (*Dei Verbum*), the Declaration on Christian Education (*Gravissimum Educationis*), and the Decree on the Instruments of Social Communication (*Inter Mirifica*) touch upon the abiding missionary tasks of the Church: worship, preaching, teaching, and, in general, communicating the Gospel to the world. The Decree on the Ministry and Life of Priests (*Presbyterorum Ordinis*), the Decree on Priestly Formation (*Optatum Totius*), the Decree on the Bishops' Pastoral Office (*Christus Dominus*), the Decree on the Appropriate Renewal of Religious Life (*Perfectae Caritatis*), and the Decree on the Apostolate of the Laity (*Apostolicam Actuositatem*) are concerned with the various groups within the Church—laity, religious, clergy, and hierarchy—who are ministerially responsible for its life and mission.

Q. 41. You emphasize the council's teaching that the Church is a mystery. Obviously you're not using the term in the sense that we speak of a murder-mystery. What exactly does it mean to refer to the Church as a mystery?

I've never been able to improve upon the definition given by the late Pope Paul VI in his opening address to the second session of the council in 1963. He said that the council was about the Church as a mystery, that is, "a reality imbued with the hidden presence of God." Thus, when we confess in the Creed our belief in the Church, we are not professing faith in the Church as an organization but in the presence of God in the Church. After all, only God is a proper object of faith. Therefore, "I believe in the Church" really means, "I believe in the God who is present and active in the Church."

The term "mystery" can perhaps be more easily understood if we substitute a more familiar theological term, "sacrament." Mystery and sacrament are practically identical in meaning. A sacrament, as some of us learned from the Baltimore Catechism many years ago, is an outward sign, instituted by Christ, to give grace. St. Augustine gave an even simpler definition: "a visible sign of an invisible grace." Sacraments are both signs and causes. They signify the saving presence of God, and they also mediate the saving presence of God. Sacraments, therefore, aren't just signs of God's redemptive will on our behalf. Sacraments actually cause the grace of salvation to be conferred on those who place no obstacle to it (for example, through mortal sin) or who are otherwise properly disposed, by faith and repentance, to the communication of God's grace.

The Church itself is a sacrament. It is both a sign and a cause of grace. In the words of the council's Dogmatic Constitution on the Church: "By its relationship with Christ, the Church is a kind of sacrament of intimate union with God, and of the unity of all humankind, that is, [the Church] is a sign and an instrument of such union and unity" (n. 1).

This new emphasis on the sacramentality of the Church, or on the Church as mystery, carries us considerably beyond the usual way of describing the Church before the council. Before Vatican II, the Church was understood primarily in institutional and organizational terms. The emphasis was on structures, hierarchies, sacred persons and objects, and individual sacraments as means of grace. In the minds of many, the parish church was a kind of spiritual filling-station. One went there to be baptized, to have one's sins forgiven, to be nourished with the Body of Christ in Holy Communion, to be confirmed, to be married, or to be prepared for death. There is a big difference, therefore, between the way the expression "sacramental Church" would have been understood in the 1950s and the way it is understood today. In the preconciliar period, the Church administered sacraments. Today, the Church is itself a sacrament. For that reason, the Church must practice what it preaches. It is not only a cause of grace. It must also and always be a credible sign of grace, that is, of the redemptive presence of God in Christ, empowered by the Holy Spirit.

Q. 42. You also stressed the point that the Church is the People of God, and not just the hierarchy or the clergy. Are you implying that Christ set up the Church as a kind of democracy where everything is decided by the people rather than by carefully selected leaders?

No. But neither is the Church an absolute monarchy or an oligarchy in which all authority is vested in one person or in a special group of persons. The Church is, according to the council, the whole People of God. It includes all of the baptized. Baptism, not ordination or religious profession, constitutes a person as a member of the Body of Christ. Ordination and religious profession only qualify the place one occupies and the responsibility one assumes within the Body of Christ. But the council insists that we're all fundamentally equal: "Everything which has been said so far concerning the People of God [that is, in Chapter II of the Dogmatic Constitution on the Church] applies equally to the laity, religious and clergy" (n. 30). The laity do not simply share in the ministerial authority or missionary responsibility of the hierarchy and clergy. That was the pre-Vatican II way of understanding the relationship between clergy and laity. Rather, the "lay apostolate…is a participation in the saving mission of the Church itself. Through their baptism and confirmation, all are commissioned to that apostolate by the Lord himself" (n. 33). This is in contrast to the earlier concept of Catholic Action, that is, the participation of the laity in the work of the hierarchy. The mission belongs not only to the hierarchy. It belongs to all of the baptized.

Does all this mean that the Church is a democracy, in the modern sense of the word? No. In fact, the Church is like no political entity, because the Church is a mystery. It is a human community, to be sure, but it is, most fundamentally, the corporate presence of God. Normal political categories cannot be applied to the Church without careful explanation and qualification. But we must remember that it would be just as wrong to refer to the Church as a monarchy or as an oligarchy as it would be to call it a democracy. On the other hand, it is closer to being a democracy than to either of the other two political models. Why? Because all baptized members are equal in dignity before God, and because all have a shared responsibility for the mission and ministries of the Church.

Q. 43. You seem to place great emphasis on the relationship between the Church and the Reign of God. I assume that the Reign of God is the same as the Kingdom of God. What does the Reign, or Kingdom, of God have to do with the Church?

Good question. The whole point and purpose of the Church is the coming of the Reign, or Kingdom, of God. As the council's Pastoral

Constitution on the Church in the Modern World states it: "The Church has a single intention: that God's kingdom may come, and that the salvation of the whole human race may come to pass" (n. 45).

The Reign, or Kingdom, of God is a biblical term for the redemptive presence of God. God reigns wherever and whenever God's will is known, honored, and obeyed. It is God's will that we should love one another. Where there is love, there is community. And where there is community, there is the Reign of God. It is also God's will that we be just to one another. Therefore, where justice is practiced, where there is a just community, there is the Reign of God, because God's will is known, honored, and obeyed.

The Reign, or Kingdom, of God was at the heart and center of Jesus' own preaching and mission. The very keynote of his ministry was proclaimed in the words, "The time is fulfilled, and the kingdom of God has come near; repent, and believe in the good news" (Mark 1:15). The council underscores this text, declaring that the Lord inaugurated the Church by preaching the good news of the coming of the Kingdom of God (Dogmatic Constitution on the Church, n. 5). Just as Jesus proclaimed the Kingdom in word, witnessed to the Kingdom in his very person, and brought about the Kingdom by his deeds, so, too, the Church, "equipped with the gifts of its founder and faithfully guarding his precepts of charity, humility, and self-sacrifice, receives the mission to proclaim and to establish among all peoples the kingdom of Christ and of God." The Church "becomes on earth the initial budding forth of that kingdom. While [the Church] slowly grows, the Church strains toward the consummation of the kingdom and, with all its strength, hopes and desires to be united in glory with its king" (n. 5).

The tendency prior to the council was to equate the Church with the Kingdom of God, with the result that the Church itself was considered to be beyond criticism or the need for fundamental reform and renewal. To find fault with the Church was the same as finding fault with the Kingdom of God—a theological impossibility. But if the Church is not yet the Kingdom of God, if it is still "straining" toward the perfection of the Kingdom, if indeed it is "at the same time holy and always in need of being purified" (n. 8), then the Church is subject to reform and renewal. Everything it does is measured against the perfection of the Kingdom of God. Until the consummation of history and the

Second Coming of Christ, the Church will always be striving and struggling, with the assistance of God's grace, to measure up to that standard.

Q. 44. You say that the Church's mission isn't limited to preaching, teaching, and the sacraments, that it includes action on behalf of justice. But doesn't this fly in the face of the council's own warnings against the Church's becoming involved in politics at the expense of its spiritual mission?

On the surface, there may seem to be a contradiction, but there isn't one. You're probably referring to article 42 of the council's Pastoral Constitution on the Church in the Modern World, which reads: "Christ, to be sure, gave his Church no proper mission in the political, economic, or social order. The purpose which he set before it is a religious one." But that isn't all the Pastoral Constitution said. In fact, that very article goes on to point out that this religious mission generates "a function, a light, and an energy which can serve to structure and consolidate the human community according to the divine law." Indeed, "the Christian view of things will itself suggest some specific solution in certain circumstances." And the document says elsewhere that the Church has "the right to pass moral judgments, even on matters touching the political order whenever basic personal rights or the salvation of souls makes such judgments necessary" (n. 76).

The Pastoral Constitution as a whole concerns the temporal order: socio-economic issues, issues of war and peace, human rights, faith and culture, Church and state. One of the most powerful statements, in opposition to the view that the Church has no role to play in matters of social justice, for example, comes in article 43 of the Pastoral Constitution. It reads in part: "Nor, on the contrary, are they any less wide of the mark who think that religion consists in acts of worship alone and in the discharge of certain moral obligations, and who imagine that they can plunge themselves into earthly affairs in such a way as to imply that these are altogether divorced from the religious life. This split between the faith which many profess and their daily lives deserves to be counted among the more serious errors of our age" (n. 43).

However, at the risk of quoting too much at you, I cannot neglect one of the most important passages in all of the council documents, arti-

cle 39 of the Pastoral Constitution. The whole article is worth study-
ing—and, by the way, there is no better commentary on the council documents than the five-volume *Commentary on the Documents of Vatican
II*, edited by the German theologian Herbert Vorgrimler—but I shall
limit myself to just a few lines. It says, "the expectation of a new earth
must not weaken but rather stimulate our concern for cultivating this
one." While "earthly progress must be carefully distinguished from the
growth of Christ's kingdom...to the extent that the former can contribute to the better ordering of human society, it is of vital concern to
the kingdom of God. For after we have obeyed the Lord, and in his
Spirit nurtured on earth the values of human dignity, human solidarity,
and freedom, and indeed all the good fruits of our nature and enterprise,
we will find them again, but freed of stain, burnished and transfigured."

Nowhere, however, is the Church's proper role in the temporal
sphere more emphatically affirmed than in the 1971 World Synod of
Bishops' document, "Justice in the World": "Action on behalf of justice
and participation in the transformation of the world fully appear to us as
a constitutive dimension of the preaching of the Gospel, or, in other
words, of the Church's mission for the redemption of the human race and
its liberation from every oppressive situation" (Introduction, para. 6).

**Q. 45. But you seem to be oversimplifying the problem. Are you
saying that the Church can involve itself in any social, economic,
or political issue without fear or danger of compromising or
violating its spiritual mission?**

Unquestionably, the problem admits of oversimplification. I hope
I haven't done that. My point is that the mission of the Church is not
limited to preaching, teaching, and the administration of the sacraments. Those are all essential to the Church's mission, but there is
more to the mission than these. The mission also includes, as "a constitutive dimension of the preaching of the Gospel," what we once called
the social apostolate and what the 1971 Synod referred to as "action on
behalf of justice and participation in the transformation of the world."

But you're right. There *are* limits to the Church's involvement in
the socio-economic and political orders. The Church can't become
enmeshed in issues that are purely political; for example, the nomina-

tion and election of candidates for political office. I have seven guide-
lines that I think are in keeping with the letter and spirit of the council's Pastoral Constitution on the Church in the Modern World, but
they are not set in stone and anyone can add to or subtract from them,
or modify them in any way he or she sees fit.

First, the issue that draws the Church into the temporal sphere
should involve public, not private, morality. It should be clearly justice-related. Second, the Church should be competent to deal with the
issue, even if it *is* justice-related and a matter of public morality. Third,
even if the Church possesses the necessary competence to deal with the
issue, it must also have the necessary resources to deal with it effectively. It can be morally counterproductive for the Church to become
involved in a public issue and then have to withdraw later on for lack
of resources. Fourth, the issue should have priority over other justice-
related issues which are competing for the Church's attention and limited resources. Fifth, the Church should always have persuasive
arguments to justify its intervention, and it should never expect or
accept any special privileges conferred by the civil authorities. The
council made this point in the Pastoral Constitution, article 76. Sixth,
the Church should never identify itself with any political party, movement, or regime, nor should it ever support or oppose candidates for
political office, even for the sake of advancing its moral position, let us
say on the issue of abortion. And seventh, the form of action the
Church takes in the public forum should not unnecessarily or unduly
polarize the Church itself. A diversity of viewpoints is to be expected,
even strong conflicts. But the Church can never forget its mission to be
a sign of Christ's presence among us, a sign that is contradicted by
sharp divisions among sisters and brothers in Christ. Therefore, while
the Church can and must propose specific solutions to specific problems, it can't make its particular proposals a litmus test of authentic
Catholic faith.

The U.S. Catholic bishops stated this last point very well in their
1983 pastoral letter, *The Challenge of Peace*: "When making applica-
tions of [universally binding moral] principles we realize...that prudential judgments are involved based on specific circumstances which can
change or which can be interpreted differently by people of good
will....However, the moral judgments that we make in specific cases,

while not binding in conscience, are to be given serious attention and consideration by Catholics as they determine whether their moral judgments are consistent with the Gospel" (n. 10).

Q. 46. You use words like "communion" and "college" when speaking about the Church. Most Catholics I know think of "Holy Communion" when they hear the word "communion," and they probably think of big bills for room and board and tuition when they hear the word "college." How is the Church a "communion" and a "college"?

The notion of "communion" is Pauline in origin. Paul concludes his Second Letter to the Corinthians with words that are familiar to us from the opening words of the Eucharist: "The grace of the Lord Jesus Christ, the love of God, and the communion of the Holy Spirit be with you all." The Church is a communion, first, because it shares in the communal life of the triune God by the power of the Holy Spirit, and, second, because the members of the Church are "in communion" with one another. That is, they are one in Christ, by the power of the same Holy Spirit. Communion, therefore, has both a vertical and a horizontal dimension. The vertical is the Church's communion with the Blessed Trinity. The horizontal is the communion of all the baptized with one another.

Nowhere is this communion more visibly or more effectively realized than in the "*Holy* Communion" of the Eucharist, when the faithful partake of Christ's body and blood and become one body thereby (1 Cor 10:16). In the early Church, for example, there was a custom of breaking off a piece of the consecrated eucharistic bread before the communion rite and sending it to neighboring churches as a visible expression of the communion that exists among churches. Eventually the word "communion" came to be used principally of the reception of the Eucharist, even though Paul's original usage was far more inclusive.

The term "college" is really an application of the word "communion." Because each local church is "in communion" with all other local churches, the universal Church is, in effect, a "college" of local churches. Collegiality, which refers to the union of all bishops with the

Bishop of Rome, is the structural expression of the communal nature
of the Church. Each bishop represents his own local church. The pope
represents the local church of Rome which, by tradition, exercises a
"primacy of love" over all other local churches and has become the
church-of-last-resort in disputed questions. By ordination bishops
become members of the college of bishops and thereby assume responsibility not only for their own dioceses but also for the whole Church
(Dogmatic Constitution on the Church, nn. 22,23).

The notion of collegiality is firmly established in the council
documents. The Dogmatic Constitution on the Church and the Decree
on the Bishops' Pastoral Office in the Church describe episcopal governance in the Church as "collegial" fifteen times and speak of the
hierarchy as unified into a "college" thirty-seven times. The Final
Report of the 1985 Extraordinary Synod of Bishops made clear the
close link between collegiality and the nature of the Church as a communion: "The ecclesiology of communion provides the sacramental
foundation of collegiality. Therefore the theology of collegiality is
much more extensive than its mere juridical aspect" (2.C.4). The communal and collegial nature of the Church are expressed in various
ways: synods of bishops, national episcopal conferences, *ad limina* vis-
its of bishops to the Holy See, and, of course, ecumenical councils.

Q. 47. You say that the Church participates in the life of the Trinity and that it is a communion animated by the Holy Spirit. But you also say that the Church is always in need of penance and renewal. Can these two statements be reconciled?

The Second Vatican Council itself held to both positions in one
and the same document. We've already pointed out the council's teaching on the communal nature of the Church in its Dogmatic Constitution
on the Church. But the council also insisted on the Church's need for
reform and renewal. How can this be? Because the Church is human as
well as divine. It is divine insofar as it is a mystery, a sacrament, a
communion in the Holy Spirit. But it is human insofar as it is composed of human beings. And since we human beings are prone to sin,
one expects this human Church to be also a sinful Church and, therefore, to be always in need of repentance and conversion.

Listen to the council's own words: "While Christ, 'holy, innocent, undefiled' (Heb 7:26), knew nothing of sin (2 Cor 5:21), but
came to expiate only the sins of the people (cf. Heb 2:17), the Church,
embracing sinners in her bosom, is at the same time holy and always in
need of being purified, and incessantly pursues the path of penance and
renewal" (n. 8). Martin Luther and his fellow Reformers would have
been astonished to learn that their battle-cry, "*Semper reformanda*
[always to be reformed]," had been incorporated into the teachings of a
later ecumenical council of the Catholic Church.

The whole council, in fact, was a reform council. It recognized
that the Church would have to be brought up to date—Pope John
XXIII used the Italian word *aggiornamento* to express the thought—if
it was to be an effective proclaimer, witness, and servant of the Gospel
for a radically new modern world. It called for change at every level: in
its liturgy and sacramental life, in the way it educates and trains its
priests for ministry, in its religious communities, in its catechetical and
liturgical portrayal of Jews, in its relationships with other Christian
churches. In every instance, whether explicitly or implicitly, the council acknowledged the failures and deficiencies of the Church itself. For
example, in the Decree on Ecumenism which called for renewed
efforts to restore the Church's lost unity, the council acknowledged that
"both sides were to blame" for the divisions that have alienated East
from West and Catholic from Protestant.

**Q. 48. You say that the laity participate directly in the mission of
the Church and not simply as sharers in the mission of the hierarchy and clergy. But isn't that the way Christ set up his Church,
with authority given directly to the Apostles and their successors
and with the rest of us in only supporting roles?**

In a word, "No." We have no evidence that Jesus ever uttered the
words, "hierarchy," "bishop," "pope," "clergy," or even "laity," for that
matter. Jesus displayed little or no interest in the manner by which his
disciples would organize themselves for their mission to preach the
good news of the coming of the Reign of God nor how they would
pass that responsibility on to others. Church structures with which we
are all familiar began to develop later, after the death of the Apostles

and the appearance on the scene of various false teachers (1 Tim 4:1-3; Titus 1:10-13; 2 Tim 3:1-9; 4:3-4). There was a growing recognition of the need for some church order. Presbyters, also known as elders, were appointed in each town and were given supervisory (literally, episcopal) functions. They monitored the religious and moral behavior of the faithful, cared for the needy out of the common goods, and ensured sound doctrine. As the older, looser charismatic structure of apostles, prophets, and teachers gave way (1 Cor 12:28), the ancient *Didache* ("teachings") urged Christians to appoint bishops and deacons. By the 90s itinerant prophets and apostles became a source of trouble and their pastoral credentials were unverifiable. So the need intensified for a more regulated structure. The so-called tripartite system (bishop-priest-deacon) came into being around this time, with the particular support of Clement of Rome who drew a clear line of authority from God to Jesus Christ to the apostles to the bishops and deacons and their successors. The awareness of a separate sacrificial Eucharist and of a separate Christian priesthood also began to appear around this time, that is, late first century, early second century. But well after the time of Jesus himself, and of the apostles, too, for that matter.

The Second Vatican Council made it very clear that the Church is the whole People of God and that, while there are different ministerial functions to be performed, every member of the Church is radically equal in Christian and human dignity. "Everything which has been said so far concerning the People of God," the council's Dogmatic Constitution on the Church declared, "applies equally to the laity, religious, and clergy." Moreover, the pastors of the Church—bishops and lower clergy—"understand that it is their noble duty so to shepherd the faithful and recognize their services [ministries] and charismatic gifts that all according to their proper roles may cooperate in this common undertaking with one heart" (n. 30).

The pre-Vatican II notion that the laity are only participants in the mission and ministries of the hierarchy, known as Catholic Action, has been supplanted by the council. "The lay apostolate," it insists, "is a participation in the saving mission of the Church itself" (n. 33). That participation comes not indirectly from the hierarchy, but rather directly from the sacraments, particularly Baptism, Confirmation, and Eucharist.

Q. 49. If Jesus didn't establish his Church as a democracy, how can we expect its leaders to exercise their God-given authority in any except an authoritarian manner?

I have already addressed the question whether the Church can be called a democracy (see Question #42, above). The issue here is the manner in which authority should be exercised in the Church, whether it be considered a democracy, a monarchy, an oligarchy, or whatever else. Fortunately, we have a model of Christian authority—in fact, the best model possible, Jesus himself. Although Jesus possessed and exercised the fullest measure of authority conceivable—forgiving sins (Matt 9:6-8; Mark 2:5-10), judging the living and the dead (Acts 10:42)—he did so always in the manner of a servant (Mark 10:45; Luke 22:27). It was precisely because he did not cling to his divinity that he became the Lord of all (Phil 2:5-11). And he charged his disciples to follow his example: "The kings of the Gentiles lord it over them....But not so with you; rather the greatest among you must become like the youngest, and the leader like one who serves" (Luke 22:25-26; John 13:14-15). His disciples, therefore, were not to be engaged in struggles for power and preferment among themselves (Matt 20:20-28; Mark 10:35-45).

Another important point to remember: the absolute power that Jesus claimed as the Son of God (Matt 28:18) was not transferred to the disciples. Not even Peter received absolute authority. In the Acts of the Apostles 1–12, where his leadership is most clearly portrayed, decisions are made not by Peter alone but by "the Twelve," or by "the apostles," or by "the church." In fact, Peter's own actions described in the tenth chapter of Acts is reviewed by "the circumcised believers" (11:1-18). His devious behavior at Antioch (where he used to eat with the Gentiles but then stopped doing so only because more conservative Jewish Christians came on the scene) elicited an open rebuke from Paul (Gal 2:11-14).

Finally, Christian authority can't be exercised in an authoritarian manner because it is vested in the whole Church and not in its leaders alone (1 Cor 12:1-28; Rom 12:3-8). There is a diversity of gifts and charisms. All must work together for the good of the whole. The basis for all authority in the Church is the Holy Spirit, and the Holy Spirit is given to all. Indeed, no one can even confess that Jesus is Lord except in the Holy Spirit (1 Cor 12:3). Therefore, all Christian authority is unique. It cannot be compared with the authority one finds in political or other social entities. It is a power existing within and for the Body of Christ. With Christ and the Church we have a whole new concept of authority. Authority is always for service, never for control or domination. It is, in the words of the council, "a true service" and a ministry (Dogmatic Constitution on the Church, n. 24).

Q. 50. How can we say that the Body of Christ includes all Christian churches when we know that Christ established only one Church?

The Second Vatican Council addressed that very question head on in its Dogmatic Constitution on the Church. Since the Church is the universal sacrament of salvation, there can only be one Church, which is at the same time holy, catholic, and apostolic. But the question is: where is this Church? The council's answer is that the Church "subsists in the Catholic Church, which is governed by the successor of Peter and by the bishops in union with that successor..." (n. 8).

On the surface, the text seems to be reiterating the traditional, preconciliar teaching on the Church; namely, that the Catholic Church is the "one, true Church" and that all of the other churches are, to one degree or another, false churches. The Body of Christ and the Catholic Church are, as Pope Pius XII taught in two of his encyclicals (*Mystici Corporis* in 1943 and *Humani Generis* in 1950), "one and the same." But when we compare the finally approved text with the previous drafts, a different picture begins to emerge.

The earlier drafts employed the copulative verb, "is." Thus, the Church "is" the Catholic Church. But the majority of council fathers objected. They argued that the verb "is" left no place in the Body of Christ for Anglican, Orthodox, Oriental, and Protestant Christians who are not in union with the Bishop of Rome. The verb "subsists in" was substituted and the text won the council's approval. Does the new language settle the problem of the relationship between the Catholic Church and the other churches? No. Does it make clear exactly how the Body of Christ is constituted? No. What it does do is leave the question open, and so it remains today.

Cardinal Jan Willebrands, former President of the Vatican Secretariat for Promoting Christian Unity and an active participant at the council itself, has insisted that we cannot fully understand the significance of this whole discussion apart from an ecclesiology of communion. Seeing the Church as a communion rather than as a society allows for degrees of unity, because communion is a matter of depth, not of quantifiable relationships. A Christian church's place in the Body of Christ, therefore, cannot be a question of all or nothing. The council's Decree on Ecumenism took this same position: "Those who believe in Christ and have been properly baptized are brought to a certain, though imperfect, communion with the Catholic Church. Undoubtedly, the differences that exist in varying degrees between them and the Catholic Church...do indeed create many and sometimes serious obstacles to full ecclesiastical communion. These the ecumenical movement is striving to overcome. Nevertheless, all those justified by faith through baptism are incorporated into Christ" (n. 3).

Q. 51. It is one thing to speak of non-Catholic churches as means of salvation, because they all believe in Jesus Christ as Redeemer and Savior. But how is it possible to include non-Christian religions as well in the work of salvation?

The council's teaching on salvation outside of Christianity is found in its Declaration on the Relationship of the Church to Non-Christian Religions, equally well-known by its Latin title, *Nostra Aetate*. The document was originally planned as a chapter in the Decree on Ecumenism, and was to be concerned principally with the Jews. However, it developed into a separate document and its theological horizons were broadened to include all non-Christian religions. The document points out that the whole human community comes from the creative hand of God, and that variations in religious faith and expression are a reflection of the diversity that characterizes humanity itself (n. 1). "The Catholic Church rejects nothing which is true and holy in these religions....[They] often reflect a ray of that Truth which enlightens all persons" (n. 2). For that reason, the council encouraged "dialogue and collaboration" with the followers of other religions in order to promote common spiritual and moral values.

The declaration praises Hinduism's emphasis on contemplation, asceticism, meditation, and trust in God (n. 2), Buddhism's recognition of the insufficiency of the material world (n. 2), and Islam's belief in the one God, its reverence for Jesus as a great prophet, its honoring of Mary, the mother of Jesus, its high moral standards, and its commitment to prayer, almsgiving, and fasting (n. 3).

The declaration also listed the many basic elements the Church has in common with the Jews, who "remain most dear to God because of their fathers, for he does not repent of the gifts he makes nor of the call he issues" (n. 4). Mutual understanding and respect are to be promoted, and Jews are no longer to be blamed, as a race, for the death of Jesus. Furthermore, the Jews are not repudiated or accursed by God, and every form of persecution and discrimination based on that false notion is to be condemned and eliminated from the practice of the Church.

Q. 52. The concept of vocation, ministry, and community are rooted in the sacrament of Baptism, which calls us to participate in the "common priesthood" of the faithful. But what does it mean to be called to "ordained priesthood," and how does one discern that call?

The Second Vatican Council's Dogmatic Constitution on the Church makes it clear that the "common priesthood of the faithful" and the "ministerial or hierarchical priesthood" of the ordained "differ from one another in essence and not only in degree." But the council also says that the two forms of priesthood are "nonetheless interrelated" and that "each of them in its own special way is a participation in the one priesthood of Christ" (n. 10).

To be called to the ordained priesthood, therefore, is not to be called to a priesthood that is totally different from the priesthood in which all of the baptized participate. Nevertheless, it *is* a distinct vocation within the Church, and there are various signs on the basis of which the candidate and the Church can make a determination—fallible though it be—of the existence of such a vocation. It is important to underscore, however, that, while the vocation comes ultimately from God, it is mediated to the individual through the Church. Therefore, it is not the individual's state of mind or state of soul that is finally determinative, but rather the judgment of the Church, expressed through various people: the diocesan bishop or other religious superior, the diocesan or religious vocation director, the seminary faculty and staff, and the parishioners with whom the individual may have worked as a deacon or in some other ministerial capacity.

Among the signs, or criteria, for deciding when a vocation to the ordained priesthood is present is the basic healthiness of the candidate, both physical and psychological. Grace builds on nature. The ordained priest must possess all those natural, human qualities that will make it possible for him to fulfill the ministry to which he has been called.

In addition to these basic human qualities, the candidate must give some evidence of being a person of supernatural virtue. He must be a person of faith, hope, and love (the theological virtues), and of prudence, justice, fortitude, and temperance (the moral, or cardinal, virtues). The candidate's faith has to be a mature faith, not a childish or naive "faith." He must be committed to Jesus Christ and the Gospel, and must have a vision of reality that has Christ at its center and as its ultimate goal. He must also be a person of hope, that is, not given to pessimism and defeatist sentiments. To be a Christian is to believe that, in spite of all known obstacles, the power of God's grace will overcome all evil in the end. The candidate must also be a person filled with love. Love by its very nature reaches out to others. A healthy self-love makes that outreach to others possible. An unhealthy self-love is narcissism. It closes one off from others, and is the antithesis of a ministerial personality.

The individual who feels called to the ordained priesthood must also exhibit the cardinal virtues. He must be a prudent person. That doesn't mean a person afraid to "rock the boat" by taking unpopular stands. Prudence is a matter of looking before one leaps, of taking counsel from people of sound judgment before embarking upon a difficult or complex course of action. The candidate must also have a sense of justice—even a passion for justice. This is surely one of the most important virtues of all, particularly in this day and age when so many lay employees of the Church, especially women, have experienced the unjust behavior of priests in parishes, schools, and other church agencies. The future priest must also be a person of fortitude, that is, of having the courage of one's moral convictions in spite of the risks of reprisal. Finally, the candidate must be, like all Christians, a person of temperance—of moderation in all things human.

Beyond these natural and supernatural qualities, the candidate must exhibit a positive (which is not to say "uncritical") sense of the Church, since every ministry is a service to the Church, requisite skills in communication (especially for preaching and presiding at liturgy), a capacity for theological study and for developing a social, political, and cultural awareness appropriate to the demands of the priestly ministry and faithful to the social teachings of the Church.

Q. 53. The reality for most Catholics is that the spirit of a parish is centered in the clergy. How does the Church move from a clergy-controlled institution to one in which the people claim and assume responsibility for their own faith?

In one sense, that problem may take care of itself, because the Catholic Church is running out of clergy. According to recent studies, seminary enrollments have dropped almost 60 percent since Vatican II, and poor retention of priests after ordination only adds to the problem. As of the mid-1990s four out of ten newly ordained priests were needed just to take over the ministries of young priests who resign from the active ministry. The other six newly ordained cannot begin to fill the vacancies created by the retirement or death of older priests. Sociologists who have studied this problem predict that the situation will only get worse. Between 1966 and 2005 the median age of priests will have increased by eight years. As the large numbers of priests ordained in the 1950s and 1960s (that includes me) reach the end of their ministries, the already limited supply of active priests will decline even more precipitously. And this at a time when the demands on priests are increasing, not decreasing. For example, Asian and Hispanic Catholics will have increased in number from 45 million in 1965 to a projected 74 million in 2005. Moreover, while the diocesan priesthood will have declined by 40 percent between 1996 and 2005, the lay population will have increased by 65 percent.

Meanwhile, lay Catholics have been assuming greater ministerial responsibilities at the parish and diocesan levels. They serve as pastoral associates, directors of religious education, youth ministers, lectors, eucharistic ministers, music ministers, ministers of hospitality, parish council members, and so forth. It is no longer the case that the common equivalent for the noun "Church" is "hierarchy" or "clergy." Laity no longer simply "attend" church, or are loyal "to" the Church, or make generous sacrifices "for" the Church, or receive the sacraments and moral guidance "from" the Church—as if the Church were only something to which the laity belong, or to which they contribute their services and resources, or from which they derive spiritual benefits. The Church is the whole People of God, laity as well as clergy and religious.

Laity are not more active in the ministerial life of the Church today simply because there is a shortage of priests. Even if there were four priests in every parish, Cardinal Bernard Law of Boston told a group of laity in 1995, lay people would still be directly involved in the life, mission, and ministries of the Church.

To be sure, there is still a long way to go before the principles of Vatican II are fully operative in the Church. But we are on the way.

Q. 54. What virtue do you feel is most important for a professional lay minister in today's Church?

That's a difficult question to answer. No one virtue seems to stand out as the most important for a lay minister in today's Church. Of course, in some pastoral circumstances one particular virtue may be more urgently needed than others, but I think that would always be a temporary phenomenon. For example, a serious issue of justice could arise in a parish or a diocesan office. A diocesan or parish employee (be she a minister or a staff person) is terminated by a new agency director or pastor in violation of her contract or without just cause. Too often other employees will look the other way out of fear of losing their own jobs if they speak up. The injustice is thereby sealed, and the person who has been fired slips quietly away, often forced to move out of the diocese and even to leave church service entirely. She has neither the money nor the physical and psychological energy to defend herself against the power and financial resources of the institutional Church. Now, in situations like that—and unfortunately these are not rare in today's Church—the one virtue which lay ministers may need more than any other is the cardinal virtue of fortitude. Other virtues would fit other circumstances.

Apart from these crisis situations, the lay minister, like the ordained, needs to be a broadly and profoundly virtuous person if she or he is to be an effective minister to others. The primary virtues are theological: faith, hope, and love. Alongside these are the cardinal, or moral, virtues: prudence, justice, temperance, and fortitude. Since every ministry is a service to and within the Church, the lay minister must be a person of the Church, at home in the Church, with a love for the people who constitute the Body of Christ. This is not to say that the lay minister should be uncritically loyal to and supportive of the pastoral leadership and policies of the Church. There are many examples of saintly Catholics—individuals like St. Catherine of Siena and St. Paul long before her—who have even confronted popes to their face. There is no necessary inconsistency between a deep and abiding Catholic faith, on the one hand, and a readiness to criticize and even to challenge church pastors, policies, and practices, on the other.

In the final analysis, balance more than anything else is required for the lay minister in today's Church.

Q. 55. On what basis is restriction of the priesthood to males justified and at what point in Church history was this dictated?

According to the *Catechism of the Catholic Church* and other official documents of the Church, the central argument against the ordination of women to the priesthood is the practice of Jesus himself and the Apostles. Jesus chose only men to be priests, and the Apostles did the same when they chose their collaborators and successors in the priestly and apostolic ministries (see n. 1577). A more recent additional argument is that the priest is the image of Christ the Bridegroom. But since only males can image a bridegroom, only males can be priests. According to this argument, the exclusion of women from the priesthood was in force from the very beginning. There is no evidence in the entire history of the Church that women have ever been ordained to the priesthood.

Pope John Paul II has been particularly emphatic about the exclusion of women from the ordained priesthood. In an apostolic letter, dated May 30, 1994, the pope declared that "the church has no authority whatsoever to confer priestly ordination on women and that this judgment is to be definitively held by all the church's faithful."

The Church's exclusion of women from the priesthood, he wrote, is not merely a matter of a changeable pastoral discipline. It is rooted in the practice of Christ himself, who did not ordain women to the priesthood, not even his Blessed Mother. The question, therefore, is not to be considered "still open to debate."

The most prominent critic of the Church's exclusion of women from the priesthood was the late Jesuit theologian, Karl Rahner (d. 1984). In a brief chapter in his *Concern for the Church* (New York: Crossroad, 1981, pp. 35-47), written in response to the 1976 declaration of the Vatican's Congregation for the Doctrine of the Faith, Rahner challenged the Vatican's central argument against women's ordination, namely, that because Christ and the Apostles did not ordain women, the Church is not authorized to ordain women. He insisted that we cannot draw any "definite and unambiguous" conclusions from Jesus' choice of men for the college of the Twelve. It is one thing to say that only men were members of the college of the Twelve, but it is quite another to say that, therefore, only men can serve as the "simple leader of the community and president of the eucharistic celebration in a particular congregation of a later period" (p. 40). Rahner argued that one also has to take into account the vast cultural differences between Jesus' time and later periods of Church history, particularly with regard to the role of women in society. It would have been sociologically unthinkable for women to have exercised pastoral leadership in first-century Jerusalem, but the reverse would be the case in late twentieth-century America or Europe, and in many other parts of the globe.

Others have pointed out that there is no biblical evidence that Jesus ordained anyone, male or female, even though subsequent tradition has regarded the Last Supper as not only the first Eucharist but also the first ordination ceremony. However, the latter is not so easy to establish as was once thought. On the other hand, the New Testament does provide some indication that women may, in fact, have been ordained to the diaconate (1 Tim 3:8-13; 5:2; Rom 16:1, where Phoebe is named as a deacon).

But the current official teaching and practice of the Catholic Church is clear, and no one—whatever one's views—can pretend that they are otherwise.

Q. 56. What would you say to women who feel that they must leave the Church to be ordained?

I would ask them to move very slowly on their decision and to consider its implications. Just as there is more to a church than its ordained members, so there is more to a church than its policy and practice regarding ordination. Thus, one could be ordained in a particular non-Catholic church and yet not really feel at home in it. It may be a church that has women clergy, but a sacramental life that is far more limited than one has been accustomed to as a Catholic. Or it may be a church that even has women bishops, but its members may represent a less expansive cultural and ethnic spectrum than one may have experienced in the Catholic Church.

On the other hand, a male priest has to be very cautious about pressing this argument too hard, lest he sound like a well-fed passerby counseling patience to a hungry beggar. Only a Catholic woman can fully understand what it means to be a woman in today's Catholic Church, and only a Catholic woman who believes herself to have a vocation to the priesthood can understand what it means to have that vocation frustrated solely because of her gender. When you add to this the long-time exclusion of girls from service at the altar and the Vatican's continued resistance to the use of gender-inclusive language in the Bible, in the liturgy, and in catechetical texts, such as the *Catechism of the Catholic Church*, it becomes easier to understand why so many Catholic women feel frustrated and even alienated by their place and role in the Church today.

Honesty, however, requires us to acknowledge that there will be no immediate change in the current teaching and discipline of the Catholic Church. As of this date, Pope John Paul II is still in office, and it is clear beyond a shadow of a doubt that there will be no change during his pontificate. Neither is there any guarantee or reasonable expectation that his immediate successor would modify the current teaching and practice. Nevertheless, one is always free to speculate and perhaps to hope. Many believe, not without reason, that women will eventually be ordained to the priesthood, and even to the episcopate, and that it will come about sometime in the twenty-first century.

In the meantime, women should continue to take advantage of every opportunity to exercise real pastoral and spiritual leadership in the Church, albeit within the confines of present ecclesiastical discipline. Such leadership has been and continues to be exercised by women heads of religious communities, hospitals, colleges and universities, high schools and elementary schools, and retreat houses, and by diocesan chancellors, parish administrators, biblical scholars, theologians, and spiritual directors.

The face of the Church may change slowly, but it changes.

Q. 57. I understand that obligatory celibacy for priests appeared several centuries after the founding of the Church. Where does celibacy fit into the definition of Catholic identity and why is it important?

You are right about the relatively late introduction of celibacy as a universal requirement for priests of the Latin rite. Although there were several local councils and individual popes in earlier centuries who strongly commended celibacy to priests, it was not until the pontificate of Gregory VII (1073-85) that a consistent pattern of observance was finally imposed, later confirmed more solemnly by the Council of Trent (1545-63). The practice in the East was confirmed much earlier, by the Trullan Synod of 692. However, the Eastern law on priestly celibacy differs significantly from the West's. In the West, neither priests nor bishops may be married, whether before or after ordination. (Exceptions have been made in recent years for former Episcopal priests who become Catholics and wish to remain as priests while married.) In the East, priests and deacons may marry before ordination, but not after. Bishops may not be married.

Celibacy fits into the definition of Catholic identity much as fish on Friday once did. It is a disciplinary practice that presently characterizes the Roman Catholic Church, setting it apart from all other churches in the Body of Christ. But, like the Friday abstinence, it is a custom that can be changed and even abolished. In that sense clerical celibacy doesn't actually fit into the definition of Catholic identity at all, because definitions pertain to what is essential. Celibacy is not at all essential to Catholicism or to its priesthood.

This is not to say, however, that celibacy is of no importance to the Church or to the Christian life generally. Celibacy was honored from the very beginning of the Church's existence—influenced no doubt by the widespread belief that the end of the world was soon to come about and, therefore, marriage was hardly a realistic option. In any case, the unmarried state was viewed as a reflection of the heavenly kingdom (Luke 20:36), where there is no marriage. But even where celibacy was recommended in the early Church, it was with the recognition that "not all can accept this teaching" (Matt 19:11-12). St. Paul advocated celibacy for those who could embrace it, but he, too, recognized that the charism was not given to all. He said it would be better for most to marry in order to avoid sin (1 Cor 7:1-9,27-28,36).

Celibacy was elevated to a kind of Christian life-style in the late third century when hermits retreated to the desert to devote themselves to prayer and penance. This movement eventually led to the development of monasticism, which further institutionalized and reinforced the practice of celibacy by priests and religious.

With the many thousands of priests leaving the priesthood after Vatican II, Pope Paul VI made the process of laicization widely available. Through much of John Paul II's pontificate, the process was severely limited and the numbers of priests receiving dispensations were sharply reduced. Just about every scientific study has shown, however, that celibacy is the single greatest cause of the precipitous decline in vocations to the priesthood and in the alarming rise in resignations therefrom. Even though the present practice of the Roman Catholic Church is clear, the issue is likely to be discussed and debated until further modifications occur.

Q. 58. In view of the priest-shortage, would you address the daily-ness, the weekly-ness, or the monthly-ness of Eucharist? What I'm asking is: How frequently does the Eucharist need to be celebrated to nurture and deepen the Christian life, and how does faith-development and witnessing to faith happen apart from the Eucharist?

The most traditional standard of frequency for the celebration of the Eucharist is weekly, in commemoration of the Lord's Resurrection on Easter Sunday (Mark 16:2). By the end of the first century, Sunday was simply known as "the Lord's day" (Rev 1:10). There is biblical evidence that in some first-century communities Sunday evening was already regarded as the most appropriate time for "the breaking of the bread" (Acts 20:7). However, there is no conclusive proof that first-century Christians celebrated the Eucharist only on Sunday. But by the mid-second century Sunday had clearly become the preferred day for the weekly eucharistic celebration. From the sixth century on the obligation to attend Mass on Sunday became a matter of church law. It has been reaffirmed in the revised Code of Canon Law which notes that the Lord's day is to be observed everywhere as the primary holy day of obligation (can. 1246).

During these earliest centuries daily Mass was not the rule. The practice probably began around the sixth century with the development of private Masses, that is, celebrated by a priest without a congregation, and particularly votive Masses, or Masses for the special needs of the faithful. The custom also developed among the faithful of making some offering for the Mass, first in the form of food products and later in the form of money. As the backlog of monetary stipends increased, the pressure to celebrate more Masses also increased. For most of the intervening centuries, in fact, private Masses came to be regarded as the rule rather than the exception. The Second Vatican Council, however, declared the communal celebration preferable to private or quasiprivate celebrations (Constitution on the Sacred Liturgy, n. 27).

There is no known tradition of a monthly celebration of the Eucharist.

Is it possible to sustain an active and committed Christian life apart from the Eucharist? Obviously it's not impossible or even extremely difficult, because many Christians who do not belong to the Catholic Church nor to other churches with a strong eucharistic tradition lead good Christian lives and effectively witness to the Gospel. The real question is whether it is possible to sustain an active and committed Christian life *in the Catholic tradition* apart from the Eucharist. The answer to *this* question would be very different. Because the Mass in the Catholic tradition is "the summit toward which the activity of the Church is directed [and] the fountain from which all her power flows" (Constitution on the Sacred Liturgy, n. 10), it would be inconceivable that a Catholic could sustain an active and committed Christian life for an extended period of time without regular participation in the Eucharist. Need it be weekly? Surely, that would be the ideal. Could a

Catholic sustain an active and committed Christian life with less-than-weekly participation in the Eucharist? Although that would not be consistent with the moral expectations of the Church, it would nonetheless be difficult to conclude that only, let us say, a monthly participation would necessarily lead to the dissolution of one's Christian life. Of course, one can always play with the numbers, but we're not dealing here with an exact science. It's a matter of conscience, first, and of prudential judgment, second.

Q. 59. A recent issue of our archdiocesan newspaper reported that present-day seminarians are more conservative and less academic than previous generations. In your travels and observations, do you find this to be true?

After the Second Vatican Council I served on a national seminary faculty for about a decade. Currently, my contacts with seminarians are limited to those who take my courses at the University of Notre Dame, but I no longer have any direct role in their formation or evaluation for ministry. Like most others, therefore, I have to rely now on scientific surveys and anecdotal evidence rather than on direct experience.

The surveys, however, have been fairly consistent in their findings over the past several years. Candidates for the priesthood do tend to be more conservative than their peers in the Church and more conservative certainly than seminarians and priests in the 1960s and 1970s. They are also less academic in the sense that they are less intellectually curious and less critical of conventional ideas about the Church, its teachings, and its disciplinary practices. This is not to say that they lack native intelligence. Some are very gifted indeed. But I.Q. is no measure of openness. An exceedingly bright person can also be ideologically rigid.

One of the most interesting changes in seminary education today is the shift in the student-teacher dynamic. Immediately before, during, and immediately after the council, some brighter, well-read seminarians found themselves theologically and pastorally at odds with many of their seminary professors, most of whom had been educated and trained well before the council. Some of these seminarians were actually better versed in contemporary theology, biblical studies, and pastoral developments than were their teachers. The seminarians were often encouraged in their thinking by a younger, more progressive minority of the faculty, fresher from their own doctoral studies in the new theology and modern critical biblical scholarship. Today, however, the situation has been reversed. Middle-aged seminary faculty members, thoroughly formed in both the letter and the spirit of the council, are regarded by many of their seminary students as radical or as inadequately loyal to the Church's hierarchical magisterium. As symbols of their resistance, some seminarians wear traditional cassocks in the seminary and the black suit and Roman collar outside the seminary. They also revert to devotional practices popular before the council, particularly those associated with the Blessed Mother. And they make much of their loyalty to the Holy Father—so much so, in fact, as to imply that fellow seminarians and faculty members with whom they disagree are not loyal to the pope.

The tension then carries over into the rectories where these seminarians are assigned as newly ordained priests. They apply the same standards of theological and doctrinal suspicion to their pastors as they did to their seminary professors. The problem, however, is even more serious in the rectory because of the closely confined living circumstances.

A report of a subcommittee of U.S. Catholic bishops several years ago referred to such tensions in its analysis of the problem of declining morale among priests. Many priests, the report said, feel themselves "caught in the middle"—between an increasingly well-educated, progressive parish, on the one side, and an increasingly conservative, play-by-the-book hierarchical establishment. How does a priest remain loyal to the hierarchy's teachings and directives while not breaking the bonds of pastoral trust with his own people? When all is said and done, the bishops' report noted, the point at issue is ecclesiology. There are often conflicting views of the nature and mission of the Church.

Q. 60. When a group of dedicated, prayerful women gather, share the word, remember Jesus, break bread, and commit themselves to proclaim and witness to his salvific action, why is that not a true Eucharist?

The safest answer is that it isn't a true Eucharist because the woman presiding at this service is not authorized by the Catholic Church to do so. Because she is not ordained, she lacks the power to change the bread and wine into the body and blood of Christ. But the safest answer is not always the best answer. The fact is that there *is* something eucharistic about such an action, even if it is not authorized and even if, in the canonical sense of the word, it is not a valid Eucharist.

What makes it eucharistic in some sense at least is that it is a gathering of Christians who open themselves to the power of God's word, who proclaim the narrative of Jesus' death and resurrection, who give thanks to God for all the gifts that have been bestowed upon them, who break bread in his name, and who share the bread and the wine with one another as a sign of their unity in Christ. To say that there is nothing eucharistic at all about such an action would require us to say the same about every eucharistic action that occurs outside the canonical confines of the Catholic Church: within Anglicanism, Lutheranism, Methodism, Presbyterianism, and so forth.

At the very least, the action of such women is sacramentally and canonically irregular. Pastorally, it is a sign of contradiction. The Eucharist is supposed to be a celebration of unity. Instead it becomes a ritual expression of division. The women who celebrate such a eucharistic action do so not because they feel themselves at one with the universal Church and with all of the local churches that constitute the universal Church. They do so because they feel alienated, cut off from the wider Church. If one is to grant some eucharistic reality to such a service, one must also be prepared to grant some schismatic reality as well. It is a painful situation for everyone, no matter what side of the debate one might take.

Q. 61. Will you please say something about the difference between an ordained Protestant minister and a priest who has received the sacrament of Holy Orders?

At this point in the history of the Catholic Church Protestant ordinations—and Anglican ordinations as well—are not recognized as valid. No Protestant or Anglican church possesses the quality of apostolic succession. Unlike the Orthodox and other Eastern-rite churches not in communion with Rome, these non-Catholic churches have done more than break the bond of unity with the pope. They have also introduced what the Catholic Church officially regards as serious doctrinal errors, particularly as they apply to the ordained priesthood. For Protestants (Anglicans pose a different problem), ordained priests are not different in kind, only in degree, from the laity, who share equally in the priesthood of Christ. Moreover, priests have no power to offer sacrifice or to forgive sins. Their only power is the power to preach. The Council of Trent in the sixteenth century directly condemned each of these views and insisted, on the contrary, that there is a clear sacramental distinction between ordained and non-ordained, that there is a divinely established sacramental priesthood with the power to offer sacrifice and to forgive sins, and that there is also a divinely constituted hierarchical structure in the Church that includes, in descending order, bishops, priests, and deacons.

The teaching of the Council of Trent remained in force, unchallenged, for the next four centuries. Not until the Second Vatican Council, in the middle of the twentieth century, did the Catholic Church's official teaching on the priesthood begin to change. It emphasized that the entire Church shares, by Baptism, in the priesthood of Christ, that the whole Church is a priestly people, that laity as well as clergy share in Christ's threefold ministry of teaching, ruling, and sanctifying. And rather than define the ordained priesthood in terms of the power to offer sacrifice and forgive sins, the council viewed the priesthood in terms of a threefold ministry of the word, of sacramental celebration, and of community leadership. Although there remains a difference in kind and not only in degree between the priesthood of the ordained and the priesthood of the faithful, the council made it clear that the priesthood of the ordained is not intended to circumvent the priesthood of the faithful but rather to serve it, to empower it, and to enable it to function (see Dogmatic Constitution on the Church, n. 30).

But we are still in the earlier years of the modern ecumenical movement. We have no idea how or where the Holy Spirit will lead us together in the next century and in the next Christian millennium.

Q. 62. What should the place of the Tridentine Mass Rite be in our modern church? Is it a relic?

The Tridentine Mass is so named because of its connection with the sixteenth-century Council of Trent. It refers to the Latin

Mass celebrated according to the ritual prescribed by the Missal of Pope Pius V in 1570. The Tridentine Mass remained in force, with only minor changes and variations, until the liturgical reforms of the Second Vatican Council were codified in the Missal of Pope Paul VI in 1970. In 1984, however, in response to many requests from more traditional Catholics who were largely, if not completely, unhappy with the liturgical reforms of Vatican II, Pope John Paul II permitted the celebration of the Tridentine Mass under certain strictly controlled conditions. Those conditions, specified in a letter from the Vatican Congregation for the Sacraments and Divine Worship, include the following: (1) There must be no connection whatsoever between the priest and people who petition for the use of the Tridentine Mass and "those who impugn the lawfulness and doctrinal soundness of the Roman Missal promulgated in 1970 by Pope Paul VI." (2) The celebration of the Tridentine Mass must take place in a church or oratory designated by the local bishop, but not in parish churches, unless in extraordinary circumstances the bishop allows it. (3) The celebration must follow the 1962 Roman Missal exactly. It must be in Latin and there is to be no intermingling of the rites or texts of the two missals.

The pope's decision was very controversial at the time. Many opposed it on the grounds that requests for the Tridentine Mass were not prompted by a genuine interest in a full and meaningful communal worship experience, but by a rejection of Vatican II's entire liturgical project. Others said it would only confuse the faithful and give many Catholics the false impression that any of the reforms of the Second Vatican Council can be circumvented if organized protests can catch the attention of sympathetic Vatican officials.

In actuality, the Tridentine Mass has not made much of an impact since it was approved for use in 1984. It is celebrated in relatively few places, by relatively few Catholics. The majority of Catholics aren't even aware that it is celebrated anywhere. If they were aware of it, they would have little or no interest in attending such a Mass. Survey after survey has shown that most Catholics are happy with the liturgical reforms of the council and would have no desire to return to the old Latin Mass. In that sense, the Tridentine Mass *is* a relic.

Q. 63. Is any one sacrament more important in the life of the Church than others?

The Council of Trent taught in 1551 that the Eucharist is the most important sacrament because it is the only one that contains within itself the very body and blood of Christ, even when the sacrament is not actually being celebrated or administered. A more modern theological explanation is that the Eucharist, of all the sacraments, most fully expresses the sacramental nature of the Church itself. According to the Second Vatican Council's Constitution on the Sacred Liturgy, the Eucharist is "the outstanding means whereby the faithful can express in their lives, and manifest to others, the mystery of Christ and the real nature of the true Church" (n. 2). It is indeed "the source and summit of the entire Christian life" (n. 11).

Everything that the Church is and is called to do is manifested in the celebration of the Eucharist. (1) The Church is a community gathered from out of the world. It is, literally, an assembly, or congregation, called by God. The first act in the celebration of the Eucharist is the gathering of the community for worship. (2) The Church is a community summoned and shaped by the word of God. At the Eucharist, during the Service of the Word, the community listens and responds to the word of God proclaimed from Sacred Scripture. (3) The Church is a community of shared goods and resources. At the Eucharist, the gifts of bread and wine are brought forward from the community to be consecrated and then shared with everyone present. (4) The Church is a community that remembers, in season and out of season, the good things that God has done for us in Christ, by the power of the Holy Spirit. The Eucharistic Prayer is a narrative of the passion, death, and resurrection of the Lord. (5) The Church is a community transformed by the presence of Christ. It is no longer simply a gathering of human beings, but it is the very Body of Christ. The Eucharist makes Christ present, body and blood, soul and divinity. By eating and drinking of the body and blood of Christ, we become more deeply one in Christ and one with Christ. (6) The Church is a community sent forth into the world to proclaim the Good News and to witness to Christ. At the end of the Eucharist, the congregation is dismissed and sent forth to carry the word and love of Christ to others. (7) The Church is a hierarchically structured community in accordance with its various missionary and ministerial responsibilities. The Eucharist is a hierarchically structured event. The priest, acting in the name of Christ, presides. Others proclaim the Scriptures. Others bring forth the gifts. Others serve at the altar. Others lead the music. Others welcome the worshipers and collect the offerings. Others directly assist the priest. Others help in the distribution of the Holy Communion.

The Eucharist is the Church in microcosm. It is the event through which the Church most fully becomes and expresses what it is and what it exists for.

Q. 64. Why do we have to move away from communal penance services, since we are a communal Church?

A communal penance service is one in which the sacrament of Reconciliation is celebrated within a liturgical assembly of more than two persons. The Book of Rites allows for two forms of communal penance. One form is for several penitents. A liturgy of the Word is held in common, but that is followed by the private confession of each penitent, with individual absolution bestowed by a single confessor. The other form is celebrated in emergencies or whenever the number of penitents disproportionately exceeds the number of available priest-confessors. Following a liturgy of the Word, there is a communal confession of sins and general absolution pronounced over the entire assembly.

What you are asking for is something else again. It would involve a communal liturgical rite, including Scripture readings, prayers, and songs, some communal (but generic) confession of sins, and a general absolution pronounced over the whole assembly by a priest. Such a rite would differ from the first form above, because there would be no individual confession of sins to a priest. It would also differ from the second form above because it would not necessarily require an emergency situation or a disproportionate excess of penitents in relation to the number of available priest-confessors. The communal penance service you obviously have in mind is one that could be held in any parish, with a moderately sized congregation, and with adequate priestly resources for individual confessions. Although many thousands of Catholics have celebrated the sacrament of Reconciliation in precisely this form, it has been explicitly disapproved by the Vatican and the bishops. Their fear is that the proliferation of such communal penance services would eventually eliminate entirely the practice of individual, or auricular, confession. Others reply that individual confessions have already declined precipitously—to the point, in fact, where they have become marginal to the life of the average Catholic. While there may be some basis for their concern, people's experience of this form has been very positive and in many instances has even led to a renewed practice of private confession. Without the communal penance service, however, the sacrament of Reconciliation may become a pastoral dead-letter in time, with only a vestige of it remaining in the introductory rite of the Eucharist.

If one recalls that there was no individual confession of sins before the sixth century, it is easier to accept the possibility that the communal penance services to which you refer will eventually be approved and become a normal feature of the Church's sacramental life.

Q. 65. What does papal infallibility mean, and how does it relate to indefectibility?

Infallibility means, literally, immunity from error. Theologically, it is a charism, or gift, of the Holy Spirit which protects the Church from fundamental error when it solemnly defines a matter of faith or morals. Notice that I said "protects the Church." Infallibility isn't given only to the pope. It is given first to the Church itself. Papal infallibility—originally defined by the First Vatican Council in 1870—is a sharing in the Church's infallibility. It is the same infallibility "with which the divine Redeemer willed his Church to be endowed" (Vatican II, Dogmatic Constitution on the Church, n. 25).

Infallibility, whether exercised by the Church through an ecumenical council or through the pope acting as earthly head of the Church, is what is known as a negative charism. It guarantees that a particular teaching is not wrong, but it does not insure that a particular teaching is the best or most appropriate way to express the truth of faith or morals.

Between Vatican I and Vatican II, the concept of papal infallibility was widely misunderstood. In the popular mind it was thought that all teachings of the pope, even casual opinions, were somehow protected by infallibility. Catholics were led to believe that they had to regard all papal statements "as if" they were infallible. This mentality was referred to as "creeping infallibility." Encyclicals, such as the one on birth control in 1968 (*Humanae Vitae*), were sometimes interpreted as if they were infallible and, therefore, beyond question or criticism, much less formal dissent. Pope Pius XII's 1950 encyclical *Humani Generis* may have given some currency to this view by stressing the definitive character of papal teachings, even in encyclicals.

The conditions under which a pope can teach infallibly were very strictly laid down by Vatican I. First, the teaching must concern some matter of faith or morals. Second, the pope must be teaching as earthly head of the universal Church. He speaks "from the chair" (*ex cathedra*) of his teaching authority. And, third, the pope must clearly intend to bind the whole Church. If these three conditions are not clearly met, canon law acknowledges that the teaching cannot be considered infallible (can. 749.3).

Indefectibility, on the other hand, refers not to a particular teaching but to the teaching mission of the Church over the long term, that is, over the entire course of the Church's historical existence. It is rooted in Christ's promise to be with the Church until the end of the world (Matt 28:30) and, in the meantime, to send the Holy Spirit to lead the Church to all truth (John 14:16). In spite of occasional or frequent errors, the Church will never fundamentally veer off the course laid down by Christ. It will remain essentially faithful and true to the Gospel.

Q. 66. How binding or obligatory is the ordinary magisterium of the Church?

Magisterium means, literally, teaching authority. The term usually applies to both the teaching authority and to the official teachers who exercise it, namely, the pope and the other bishops. In that case, it is best to modify the noun by the adjective, "hierarchical," because the term also has wider meanings. It can apply to teachers whose teaching authority is rooted in their scholarly competence, such as theologians and biblical scholars, as well as teachers whose authority is rooted in their pastoral office. In its widest meaning, magisterium applies to the whole Church, which, according to Vatican II, shares in Christ's threefold ministry of teaching, ruling, and sanctifying (Dogmatic Constitution on the Church, n. 30).

Since the Church is called to proclaim, profess, and witness to the Gospel of Jesus Christ, it must be a community united in the faith received from Christ and the apostles. When conflicts or new questions arise, as inevitably they have, the unity of the Church requires some authoritative voice to resolve or address them. It is not that the bishops are above the word of God, but it is their particular ministry to see to it that the word is properly interpreted and proclaimed.

The "ordinary" magisterium is the non-definitive, non-dogmatic, non-infallible teaching authority exercised by the pope and the other bishops. The pope exercises his ordinary magisterium through encyclicals, apostolic letters, important speeches, and so forth. Bishops exercise their ordinary magisterium in international, national, and regional synods, in ecumenical councils, in official statements and pastoral letters of national episcopal conferences, and in various forms at the diocesan level. Is such teaching binding or obligatory? Yes, but not in the same way that the extraordinary magisterium is binding or obligatory, and also not in the same way that the ordinary universal magisterium is binding or obligatory. Nevertheless, even non-definitive, non-infallible teachings call for a response of "religious submission (or respect)." It is an attitude of willingness to accept the teaching or at least to make a good-faith effort to do so. If the latter effort should fail, it does not necessarily follow that the individual believer has withheld "religious submission (or respect)."

Q. 67. What do you mean by ordinary universal magisterium?

This is a relatively recent concept (the first known reference was by Pope Pius IX in 1863, later reinforced by Vatican I in 1870) and it still remains somewhat unclear. Essentially it refers to the consensus of the whole college of bishops in the exercise of their ordinary teaching authority, or magisterium. It is ordinary, therefore, because there is no solemn, or dogmatic, pronouncement given in an ecumenical council. And it is universal because the teaching reflects the consensus of the worldwide episcopate, and not simply of a national episcopal conference, a synod, or a large group of individual bishops.

The Second Vatican Council's Dogmatic Constitution on the Church put it this way: "Although the individual bishops do not enjoy the prerogative of infallibility, they can nevertheless proclaim Christ's doctrine infallibly. This is so, even when they are dispersed around the world, provided that while maintaining the bond of unity among themselves and with Peter's successor, and while teaching authentically on a matter of faith or morals, they concur in a single viewpoint as the one which must be held conclusively" (n. 25). The clearest and most balanced analysis of this text is provided by Francis A. Sullivan, S.J., for more than 30 years Professor of Theology at the Gregorian University in Rome, in his book *Magisterium: Teaching Authority in the Church* (Paulist Press, 1983, pp. 123-27).

The issue of the ordinary universal magisterium first came to a head in 1968 with the publication of Pope Paul VI's encyclical on birth control, *Humanae Vitae*. A few theologians who were strongly supportive of the pope's encyclical insisted that its central teaching on artificial contraception was infallible because it reflected the belief and constant teaching of the worldwide episcopate. Ironically, the liberal theologian Hans Küng also regarded the encyclical as infallible, at least by the Church's own standards—but wrong. Therefore, he concluded, there is no such thing as infallibility, only indefectibility. Most theologians, then and since, have not regarded *Humanae Vitae* as an infallible teaching.

Q. 68. How does the "sensus fidelium" relate to the magisterium of the Church?

Sensus fidelium literally means "the sense of the faithful." It is sometimes rendered as *consensus fidelium* ("consent of the faithful") and *sensus fidei* ("the sense of faith"). It is a reminder that the Holy Spirit is present and active in the whole Church, not only in the hierarchy. The whole Church is the Temple of the Holy Spirit, anointed and animated by the Spirit (1 John 2:27). Therefore, the faith of the People of God is an important criterion of orthodoxy, alongside others. In other words, the whole Church (including the laity) is a teaching Church, and the whole Church (including the hierarchy) is a learning Church.

The concept of *sensus fidelium* is found, at least implicitly, in the early Fathers of the Church who insisted that church teaching can never contradict the universal and corporate faith of the Church. A fifth-century monk, St. Vincent of Lérins, is most often identified with this view. Tradition, he wrote, is "what has been believed everywhere, always, and by all" (*quod ubique, quod semper, quod ab omnibus*). He was also careful to point out, however, that tradition is subject to growth and interpretation. In modern times Cardinal John Henry Newman elaborated upon this teaching in his famous essay of 1859, *On Consulting the Faithful in Matters of Doctrine*, and the French Dominican theologian Yves Congar developed it even further in his *Lay People in the Church*, just prior to Vatican II.

Vatican II itself affirmed this teaching: "The body of the faithful as a whole, anointed as they are by the Holy One, cannot err in matters of belief" (Dogmatic Constitution on the Church, n. 12). This quality is manifested when the whole Church, guided by the Holy Spirit, "shows universal agreement in matters of faith and morals." While this doesn't mean that every common belief of the faithful is true, it does mean that the experience of the faithful is a source for theology and for doctrine, and that the faithful should, therefore, be consulted in the formulation of church teaching.

Of course, it isn't an easy matter to determine the *sensus fidelium*. Does one do so through scientific polls and surveys? How widely should such surveys be done? How does one differentiate among various countries, regions, and cultures? On the subject of birth control, for example, are "the faithful" to be consulted only those who are married and of child-bearing age, or are "the faithful" to include the unmarried, widows and widowers, and those past their child-bearing years? As with the concept of ordinary universal magisterium, the task of determining the *sensus fidelium* is an inexact science, often subject to widely varying interpretations.

Q. 69. Doesn't this notion of "sensus fidelium" also have something to do with the concept of reception of doctrine?

Yes. A doctrine, a liturgical directive, or a disciplinary decision of the official Church does not become part of the faith and practice of the people until it has been "received" by them and made their own. A doctrine, directive, or decision is said to be received when it actually changes the thinking and behavior of those to whom it is directed. The concept of reception here is active, not passive. The mere physical reception of something isn't equivalent to reception in the theological sense of the word. For example, we receive all kinds of things in the mail. Some we toss out immediately. Others we read, hold onto for a while, and then dispose of. Others we reply to—if only to tell the other party we're not interested. Still others we read and reply positively to, such as when we accept an offer for a trial subscription to a magazine. Only in this last instance is there true reception.

Reception in the Church does not mean "taking a vote" and then deciding on the truth or validity of a teaching, directive, or decision on that basis alone. It is more complex and more mysterious (in the sense of sacramental) than that. Indeed, in the New Testament reception is an act of faith. It has to do with accepting God's word (Mark 4:20), Christ's message (Rev 2:41), and the Gospel (1 Cor 15:1). It also concerns the acceptance of Jesus and God by accepting those whom Jesus and God have sent (Matt 10:40; John 13:20). The whole process of acceptance, or reception, is governed and guided by the Holy Spirit (1 Cor 2:10-16).

The ancient creeds, liturgies, and conciliar decrees gained general recognition and authority by means of their reception by the Church at large. The formation of the canon of Sacred Scripture (which books belong in the Bible and which do not) was also the product of reception. It was only after centuries of regular usage in teaching, in worship, in prayer, and in study that the Church came gradually to recognize which books were inspired and which were not.

Although the theological concept of reception is as old as the Church itself, and although other Christian traditions, especially the Orthodox and the Anglican, have never really lost it, we Catholics have only recently recovered it in our own theology. When did we "lose" it? It's impossible to identify any specific point in history, but the transition from the first to the second Christian millennium is as good a guess as any other. It was at this time, especially with the pontificate of Gregory VII (1073-85), that the Catholic Church shifted to a more monarchical form of governance centralized in the pope and the Roman Curia. The concept of *reception* by the faithful gave way to *obedience* by the faithful to teachings and decrees from on high.

The concept of reception does not invalidate the teaching authority of the pope and the other bishops, but it does remind us that the whole Church is, and must be, meaningfully engaged in that teaching process since the whole Church is the People of God and the Temple of the Holy Spirit. Even in the case of infallible definitions, the role of the faithful is indispensable: "To the resultant definitions the assent of the Church can never be wanting, on account of the activity of the same Holy Spirit, whereby the whole flock of Christ is preserved and progresses in unity of faith" (Dogmatic Constitution on the Church, n. 25).

Modern examples of reception include the generally positive effects of the Second Vatican Council's teachings on the thinking and practice of the postconciliar Church. A modern example of non-reception, or at least of partial non-reception, is the widely negative response to *Humanae Vitae* by Catholic married couples of child-bearing age.

Q. 70. We don't hear much any more in our churches about the ecumenical movement, and ecumenical celebrations are few. What is the present state of the ecumenical movement?

The ecumenical movement is still very much alive. In a sense, the lack of explicit attention to it may be a sign of its success. The various Christian churches simply take for granted now their oneness in Christ. They pray together, collaborate on social ministry projects, exchange pulpits, read each other's theological and spiritual books, and study together in seminaries and divinity schools, and in adult education programs. However, there is another, more negative side to the ecumenical situation today. After many years of officially sponsored ecumenical dialogues and in spite of several important joint recommendations for intercommunion and the mutual recognition of ordained ministries, no real structural changes have occurred between and among the several churches. Intercommunion is still practiced only unofficially at the individual level, for example, in the reception of Communion by non-Catholics at Sunday Mass or at weddings and funerals, and the occasional reception of Communion by Catholics at non-Catholic services. But there is still no formal church-to-church celebration of the Eucharist or Lord's Supper. We have made even less progress in the matter of the mutual recognition of ordained ministries.

Apart from pulpit exchanges and friendly personal relationships between clergy, we are no closer to officially recognizing Anglican or Lutheran orders, for example, than we were at the time of the Second Vatican Council when ecumenical euphoria was at its height.

Another point to keep in mind is that during the relatively lengthy pontificate of John Paul II, beginning in 1978, the Vatican's ecumenical focus shifted from the Protestant West to the Orthodox East. John Paul II reaffirmed and reinforced policies that the Protestant West finds unacceptable, namely, clerical celibacy and the prohibition against the ordination of women. At the same time, these stances have been reassuring to the more conservative Orthodox in the East. However, despite the pope's efforts to build new and stronger spiritual bridges between Catholics and Orthodox, Catholic dogmas on papal primacy and papal infallibility remain a serious obstacle to reunion. And, although it is not usually said publicly, John Paul II's restoration of a more centralized papal form of governance of the universal Church and his corresponding reduction of the role of national episcopal conferences has been troubling for the Orthodox, who are more accustomed to a synodical and conciliar form of church governance. However, in his 1995 encyclical, *Ut Unum Sint* ("That they may be one"), Pope John Paul II explicitly invited non-Catholic Christians to enter a dialogue with him on the exercise of the papal office.

One of the other interesting ecumenical developments in recent years, especially in the United States, is the new alliance formed between conservative Catholics and evangelical and fundamentalist Protestants, not on doctrinal issues but on moral and social issues such as abortion, homosexuality, pornography, and feminism.

But we are still in the early stages of the modern ecumenical movement and it is impossible to predict the direction it will take in a new century and at the beginning of a new Christian millennium.

Q. 71. My son married a Protestant in the Protestant Church and the ceremony was performed by a minister. Is my son still allowed to receive the sacraments in the Catholic Church?

It depends. Many Catholics are allowed to be married in a Protestant church and by a Protestant minister. But they must have the

Church's (specifically, the bishop's) permission to do so. That permission is called a dispensation. In this case, it would be a dispensation from what is known as "canonical form." Canonical form refers to the requirement that all Catholics be married before a properly authorized Catholic minister and two witnesses. Usually the minister is a priest or deacon who is authorized to perform marriages by virtue of his office or by delegation from the pastor or the bishop. Church law also allows a lay minister to officiate if the bishops of a country petition the Holy See for such authorization. In inter-faith marriages, that is, marriages between a Catholic and a non-Christian, Catholics may receive a dispensation from canonical form and marry in any public place.

The question is whether your son, or any Catholic in similar circumstances, is free to marry. If he is not free to marry because of a previous valid marriage that has not been, or cannot be, annulled, then the questions of where the second marriage takes place and who performs the ceremony are moot. The second marriage would not be recognized as canonically valid by the Catholic Church.

As to the question of your son's being allowed to receive the sacraments: The answer is clearly "Yes" if his marriage in the Protestant church was conducted with the permission of the Church, that is, with proper dispensation from canonical form. But the answer is just as clearly "No" if your son was not free to marry, whether in a Catholic Church or in any other forum. If the latter is the case, your son should at least inquire into the possibility of rectifying the situation by appealing to his diocesan marriage court. There may be canonical grounds for annulling his prior marriage, if indeed there was one.

Before the Second Vatican Council, if an American Catholic married outside the Catholic Church, as your son did, that Catholic would be automatically excommunicated, according to church law in force in the United States since the nineteenth century. That law has been abolished. A Catholic who marries outside the Church now, without proper authorization, may commit a sin—objectively at least—but that Catholic is still a member of the Church. Whether that Catholic may also receive the sacraments is another question. It is a matter of conscience that should be worked out between the individual and his or her spiritual director or confessor. We know, in fact, that many thousands of divorced-and-remarried Catholics receive Communion today, and in good conscience.

Q. 72. Could you comment on the goal of the recent effort to bring understanding between Catholics and Jews?

The high-point of recent Catholic efforts to develop a more positive mutual understanding between Catholics and Jews was the passage of the Second Vatican Council's Declaration on the Relationship of the Church to Non-Christian Religions, better known by its Latin title as *Nostra Aetate* ("In Our Age"). The document declares that "the Jews still remain most dear to God because of their fathers, for he does not repent of the gifts he makes nor of the calls he issues" (n. 4). The declaration directly challenges the prejudices that all Jews are somehow responsible for the death of Jesus and, therefore, are to be regarded for all time as "Christ-killers." What happened to Jesus, the declaration insists, "cannot be blamed upon all the Jews then living, without distinction, nor upon the Jews of today. Although the Church is the new people of God, the Jews should not be presented as repudiated or cursed by God, as if such views followed from the holy Scriptures" (n. 4). The principle, the council pointed out, should always be reflected and followed in the Church's catechetical instruction and in its preaching.

Indeed, the Church "deplores the hatred, persecutions, and displays of anti-Semitism directed against the Jews of any time and from any source" (n. 4). We cannot pretend to love God if we reject our Jewish brothers and sisters who are created in the image of God (n. 5). Not surprisingly, the declaration has had a very positive impact on Catholic-Jewish relations since the council, promoting theological dialogue, joint prayer, and collaboration in social ministry.

Which is not to say, however, that there haven't been serious problems and misunderstandings along the way. Although Pope John Paul II has been one of the most active popes in history in terms of efforts to reach out sympathetically to Jews, his decision to grant an audience to the former head of the United Nations and then President of Austria, Kurt Waldheim, was a source of much pain for Jews. Waldheim had just been exposed as having had connections with the Nazis during the Second World War and was treated as a political pariah by almost every country in the world. The slow pace of moving a new convent of nuns away from the former death camp at Auschwitz in Poland was another source of disaffection between Jews and the Vatican. But Pope John Paul II eventually saw to it that the convent was moved and the Waldheim incident was quickly forgotten after the pope received a number of Jewish leaders at the Vatican. In the meantime, he has visited the main Jewish synagogue in Rome and conducted a joint prayer service with Rome's chief rabbi, and held a commemorative concert in the Vatican on the occasion of the fiftieth anniversary of the Holocaust. In 1992 the first steps were taken that led eventually to the formal recognition of the State of Israel by the Vatican.

However, more than the council or the pope, the real basis for positive relations between Catholics and Jews is our common Jewish heritage and the fact that Jesus, the one we Catholics proclaim as Lord and Savior, was himself a Jew and remained a Jew to the end.

Q. 73. How do I, a woman in ministry in the Catholic Church, respond to those men—priests—who simply pay lip-service and yet won't change the sexist language in the Scriptures, for example, or won't do anything to advance the equality of women in the Church?

This is an extremely difficult question to answer because pastoral situations differ so much from place to place. And so do the personalities involved. If I could assume that the priest or priests in question are basically healthy, secure, non-defensive, open-minded human beings, I would advise you to initiate some form of dialogue with him or them. If other women (and men) on the parish's ministerial team have similar problems with the pastor, they should also be part of the dialogue. He should be invited to take a new and different look at the situation and to try to understand how and why the issue is so important to you. In turn, you should make it easy for him to communicate his own point of view on the matter. Hear him out, before interrupting with rebuttals. Once all the views are laid out on the table, some member of your group who is adept at group dynamics should guide the conversation and discussion along the most productive and least inflammatory paths. Neither side may come away with everything it wanted, but compromise and accommodation are better than defiance and polarization. There will always be another day when both sides can restate their concerns and when some further adjustment of the original compromise can be effected.

The problem, of course, is that in too many instances women in ministry such as yourself do not have the luxury of working with a new pastor (it's usually a new pastor, isn't it?) who is healthy, secure, non-defensive, and open-minded. You have a problem precisely because he lacks those qualities. He is often clerical, authoritarian, closed-minded, and uptight, especially in his dealings with strong professional women. (I can "see" many women nodding in agreement as they read these words.) What do you do then? Well, there isn't a great deal anyone *can* do, other than form strong alliances within the ministerial team and with other influential members of the parish, especially members of the parish council. Sometimes, a person will act nobly in spite of his proclivities to act otherwise, simply because he knows his options are limited. If he has to choose between asserting his authority and alienating just about everybody that counts, a sensible man will back off. If that is the case, give him a face-saving out so that he won't suffer unnecessary embarrassment or humiliation before his new parish. There are ways of making concessions on matters that don't count for very much, while holding firm on matters that do count.

There are signs of hope, however. First, women ministers are more assertive than in the past. They are more conscious of their own dignity and status as bona fide ministers of the Church, and they also know that the Church desperately needs them. Indeed, more than 80 percent of all ministers today are women. It should be obvious to any reasonable person, including clergy, that the Church cannot afford to alienate its women ministers any more than it may already have done. Second, many others in the Church are becoming increasingly vocal in their support of women in ministry and in support of such efforts as introducing the use of non-sexist language in liturgy and catechetics. The 1995 Congregation of the Society of Jesus issued an extraordinarily supportive document on women in the Church (see *Origins*, April 13, 1995), and the Catholic Biblical Association has been in the lead in urging the use of gender-inclusive language in the Bible.

Q. 74. Do you believe if women were "up and down the hierarchical ladder," the Church's teaching on abortion would be more nuanced?

The deeper question is: Is the way the Church formulates its teaching affected by the teaching process itself and particularly by the breadth of participation in that process? The answer to that deeper question is unequivocally "Yes." We have no better examples, in fact, than the two pastoral letters issued by the U.S. Catholic bishops in 1983 and 1986 respectively. The first, "The Challenge of Peace" (1983), addressed the complex issue of nuclear warfare and the stock-piling and use of nuclear weapons. The second, "Economic Justice for All" (1986), applied Catholic social teaching to the U.S. economy. In both instances, the letters were fashioned in the open, with full public hearings at which experts and interested parties representing a mix of specializations and viewpoints were invited to testify. Drafts were circulated and criticisms and suggestions were solicited, computerized, and, as far as possible, incorporated into a subsequent draft. The final draft in each instance was debated, amended, and passed in open session, with the media and other parties present. So credible and so broadly participatory was the process, that the final documents gained a large and wide measure of respect even from those who differed with many of their conclusions. Unquestionably, that broadly participatory process affected the final outcome. Most observers close to the scene would have to acknowledge that the pastoral letters were much better for having gone through that type of process.

If that was clearly the case with the two pastoral letters, why would it not also be the case with any church teaching, including one on the morally sensitive issue of abortion? Archbishop Rembert Weakland of Milwaukee recognized this truth when, several years ago, he organized six different public meetings in his archdiocese to hear the views of women on this issue. He did not pre-select the participants. The women could be strongly pro-life or strongly pro-choice, with many shades of difference in between. They could be married, single, or divorced. They could be lay or religious. They could be old or young or middle-aged.

By all accounts, the meetings were successful. Archbishop Weakland and his associates listened carefully and patiently. They were not there to challenge or to contradict what they heard. They did not view their responsibility primarily as one of defending the official teaching of the Church. They listened. And they listened some more. Some vehemently criticized the archbishop for having conducted these meetings. They charged that, by his silence, he was giving legitimacy to views at odds with the official teaching of the Church. Such is the price one pays for inviting people to speak their minds openly and freely, without fear of instant rebuttal or eventual reprisal.

The U.S. Catholic bishops attempted the same course of action in the early stages of the ill-fated pastoral letter on women in the Church. They, too, invited women of all backgrounds and points of view to appear before a special committee and express their views on the role and place of women in the Church. It was probably the most valuable part of the whole nine-year process. Unfortunately, some bishops concluded that it would be imprudent to incorporate such a wide divergence of views in any official document. Diversity and pluralism are, for some, a sign not of vitality but of disunity. And so the women's testimony was suppressed in the next draft and was never carried forward to the end of the process. The final draft of the pastoral letter received a majority of affirmative votes, but not the necessary two-thirds. And so it was shelved.

One likes to think that if there were a broadly participatory process within the Church to reformulate (not necessarily to change fundamentally) the official teaching on abortion, it would produce a formulation that would have wider support, even from pro-choice Catholics, than the present formulation. Both sides would be challenged to rethink their hard-and-fast positions. Who knows what the Holy Spirit might accomplish in such an open and broadly participatory process?

Q. 75. Does Catholic inclusiveness have room for gay and lesbian Christians in your view? Specifically, what is your reaction to the Vatican's attitude toward civil rights legislation for gays and lesbians?

Unmistakably, yes. Gay and lesbian Christians are as much a part of the Body of Christ as are heterosexual Christians. The general principle applies, of course, to gay and lesbian Catholics in their specific relationship to the Catholic Church. Sexual orientation does not determine one's relationship to Christ and his Church. Sexual behavior is another matter. However, not even sexual behavior places one outside the Church, regardless of its moral quality. Mortal sin separates us from union with God, at least temporarily, but it does not separate us from union with the Church unless it is one of the few mortal sins to which the penalty of excommunication is attached, for example, laying violent hands on the pope or desecrating the Eucharist. Neither a homosexual orientation nor homosexual behavior is grounds for excommunication from the Church.

The official teaching of the Church, recapitulated in the *Catechism of the Catholic Church*, is that homosexual acts are intrinsically disordered, because they are contrary to the natural law. On the other hand, the *Catechism* concedes that a homosexual orientation is not a matter of choice. Accordingly, the Catholic Church insists that gays and lesbians be treated with respect and sensitive pastoral care, and that all signs of unjust discrimination should be avoided.

In July 1992 the Vatican's Congregation for the Doctrine of the Faith issued a set of observations concerning various legislative proposals, primarily in the United States, that would make discrimination against gays and lesbians illegal (see *Origins*, August 6, 1992). The Vatican is concerned with gay rights ordinances because of the alleged "danger that legislation which would make homosexuality a basis for entitlements could actually encourage a person with a homosexual orientation to declare his homosexuality or even to seek a partner in order to exploit the provisions of the law." Although the Congregation reiterated the Church's view that homosexuals should not be subjected to violence or abuse of any kind because of their sexual orientation, the content and tone of the text seem to place the Vatican on the side of politically conservative forces which oppose anti-discrimination legislation on principle. The Vatican leaves open the possibility, for example, that homosexual partners could legitimately be excluded from housing, from the armed services, from functioning as adoptive or foster parents, and from employment as teachers and athletic coaches. This raises, of course, the even larger issue of the relationship between the moral law and the civil law—an issue, however, that brings us beyond the more explicitly ecclesiological aspects of the question you posed.

Q. 76. In your opinion, what can be done to bring the spirit of justice and Catholic social teaching generally into the life of the parish at all levels?

I can think of no issue that poses a greater threat to the credibility of the Church in our time than the manner in which the Church treats its own employees, at both ministerial and staff levels. How justice and the social teaching of the Church can be enforced at the parish level is a difficult question to answer because there are at present no mechanisms of enforcement. It seems to depend primarily on the bishop, the pastor, the hospital administrator, the school principal, or the agency director—or a combination thereof. If they are just, the employees will be treated justly. If they are not just, the employees are not likely to be treated justly.

For starters, however, all employees of the Church—be they ministerial or staff personnel—should be aware of the official teaching of the Church as it applies to them. In the one-hundred-year history of Catholic social teaching, there have been only two official documents that have addressed the issue of justice *inside* the Church: the 1971 World Synod of Bishops' "Justice in the World," and the 1986 pastoral letter of the U.S. Catholic bishops, "Economic Justice for All: Catholic Social Teaching and the U.S. Economy."

The synodal document, "Justice in the World," declared: "While the Church is bound to give witness to justice, it recognizes that anyone who ventures to speak to people about justice must first be just in their eyes. Hence we must undertake an examination of the modes of acting and of the possessions and life style found with the Church itself. Within the Church rights must be preserved. No one should be deprived of his or her ordinary rights because he or she is associated with the Church in one way or another." The document insists specifically that those who serve the Church by their labor—laity, religious, and clergy alike—"should receive a sufficient livelihood and enjoy that social security which is customary in their region." Lay people, and women in particular, must also be given a meaningful share of responsibility and participation in the life and mission of the Church.

The U.S. Catholic bishops were even more emphatic and detailed in their 1986 pastoral letter, "Economic Justice for All" (see especially paras. 347-353). The following sentence was italicized in the letter:

"All the moral principles that govern the just operation of any eco-nomic endeavor apply to the church and its agencies and institutions; indeed the church should be exemplary" (n. 347). Throughout this sec-tion of the pastoral, the bishops quoted liberally from the 1971 synodal document, "Justice in the World." Among the rights that the bishops underscored is the right to form labor unions or other associations and to bargain collectively through them. Bishops and other church employers are not to refuse to bargain with their employees simply because they do not like the bargaining agents. Moreover, church employers are to be especially careful about salary inequities between women and men and about the concentration of women at the lower end of the wage scale (n. 353).

If our eyes and ears and hearts are open to the grievances voiced by so many church employees (the overwhelming majority of whom are women), then we can understand why this is one of the gravest problems the Catholic Church faces today. The Church is a sacrament, which means that it must visibly signify what it is invisibly. When the Church acts unjustly, especially against its own members, it contradicts the sacred reality that it embodies and is called to signify to the world. The issue of internal justice, therefore, touches directly on the nature and mission of the Church.

Q. 77. What do you see as a catalyst for the changes you foresee in the Church, especially in the areas of social teaching and social justice? I could use a small ray of hope.

Ideally, the changes will come about because those who hold decision-making authority in the Church will increasingly recognize that Catholic social teaching is meant to be applied to the internal life of the Church itself. They will also see that the sacramentality of the Church requires us to practice what we preach and thereby to signify to the world who we are spiritually and invisibly, namely, the Body of Christ and the Temple of the Holy Spirit. Practically, however, this is not likely to be the case. What is more likely to stimulate change is the continued decline in vocations to the priesthood and religious life as well as the growing alienation of women from the Church. The fewer priests and nuns, the greater the need for lay ministers. The fewer women there are available for lay ministry, the greater the likelihood that essential ministerial tasks will simply not get done. Women, after all, constitute more than 80 percent of the present ministerial force of the Catholic Church. No organization can afford to alienate so vital a part of its regular work-force.

Given the Catholic system of church governance, pastoral leadership at all levels is of crucial importance in the resolution (or worsening) of any problem such as this. Although Pope John Paul II and his immediate predecessors have been vigorous advocates of justice and enlightened promoters of the Church's social teaching, none of them has made the explicit connection between justice in the Church and justice outside the Church. A future pope could make that connection dramatically, and that would affect the life of the Church at every level, including the parish. In an individual diocese, a bishop can have the same effect, albeit in a far more limited way than the pope. And an individual pastor can make things substantially better (or substantially worse) because, in the final analysis, his decisions and his attitudes affect the life of a church employee more directly than any other pastoral leader. Outside the parochial and diocesan systems, there are the hospital administrators and other heads of church agencies and institutions. The same dynamic applies to them as to the pope, the bishop, and the pastor. And that is both the strength and the weakness of the Catholic system of governance. Good leaders can make good things happen immediately. But bad leaders can make bad things happen just as quickly, and with little or no recourse on the part of the aggrieved parties.

Is there reason for hope? Of course, there is. Catholics generally are more enlightened about issues of this sort than they were only a decade or so ago. Women in particular are more conscious of their dignity and rights within the Church. And there is a greater freedom—although still too little exercised—in the Church to call attention to violations against justice in parishes, dioceses, hospitals, schools, and other Catholic institutions. A few Catholic periodicals and at least one lay-edited national newspaper have been effective in this regard. As in society at large, an aroused citizenry is always the best antidote to corruption and abuses of power.

Q. 78. I am a lay businessman. On the issue of just wages within the Church, isn't it the case that the real problem in the Church is our lack of willingness to share our material wealth with those in greater need? How can we teach responsibility to the average person in this area of sharing or tithing?

No Christian could possibly take exception to your underlying argument that we have to be more generous and self-sacrificial in the matter of personal wealth and possessions. After all, for whom is the message of sharing more appropriate than for Christians? Unfortunately, the economic problems that society at large and the Church in particular face cannot be solved totally by private initiatives and private charities. Politically conservative individuals prefer that approach because it means less governmental involvement in social problems and, therefore, less taxes for themselves. But that is not the official position of the Church itself.

In his 1991 encyclical *Centesimus Annus*, Pope John Paul II characterized as "an elementary principle of sound political organization" that "the more that individuals are defenseless within a given society, the more they require the care and concern of others, and in particular the intervention of governmental authority" (n. 10). And against the view that all economic problems can be solved if market forces and private initiatives are allowed free play, without interference from government, the pope insisted that "the market be appropriately controlled by the forces of society and by the state so as to guarantee that the basic needs of the whole of society are satisfied" (n. 35). Finally, "It is not merely a matter of 'giving from one's surplus,' but of helping entire peoples which are presently excluded or marginalized to enter into the sphere of economic and human development. For this to happen," the pope declared, "it is not enough to draw on the surplus goods which in fact our world abundantly produces; it requires above all a change of lifestyles, of models of production and consumption, and of the established structures of power which today govern societies" (n. 58).

The fact of the matter is that private charities cannot possibly meet the legitimate needs of every member of society. Private charity is essential as a supplement to governmental action and also as a moral imperative of Christian faith, but it is not enough by itself. And that is what Pope John Paul II, and Catholic social teaching generally, have consistently pointed out.

Regarding tithing, or the setting aside of a tenth of one's income for sacred purposes, the Catholic Church, unlike some fundamentalist Protestant churches, has never commended, much less imposed, the practice on its members. Although practiced in Old Testament times, tithing is only mentioned in passing in the New Testament.

Q. 79. In many gatherings of Catholics I've been at, for lectures and the like, the average age of most people seems to be over fifty. How do we reach the youth of our community and bring them into the full and active life of the Church?

Many people in the Church have a far surer grasp of the situation and experience of Catholic youth than I do, although my years as a professor in two major Catholic universities—Boston College and Notre Dame—have perhaps given me some limited insight into the thinking and behavior of many younger Catholics. My answer, however, is necessarily general in scope.

First, I agree with your impression about Catholic gatherings. Although we hear a lot these days about a spiritual hunger and resurgence among young people, manifested, for example, in the many thousands who came to see and pray with the pope during World Youth Day in Denver a few years ago, younger Catholics tend to engage in religious activities with other young people rather than as part of mixed groups. That leaves middle-aged and senior Catholics with the mistaken impression that there isn't much of a future for the Church since so few young Catholics seem to be directly involved with it or even interested in it.

Second, based on my teaching experience at Boston College and Notre Dame, I would say that many younger Catholics are still vitally interested and engaged in the Church, especially liturgically through residence hall liturgies in which they take a very active part. However, when they return to their parishes during vacation periods and after graduation, they find too wide a gap between their university and parochial experiences, and so they drift away from Mass and the sacraments, at least until marriage and the raising of a family. Then, for the sake of the children, they tend to return to the regular practice of their faith. I think you will agree that this is a very common experience, not only for Catholic university graduates but for other young Catholic adults as well.

Third, because young Catholics experience "moral growing pains" that are an inevitable part of human maturation, they look instinctively to others for guidance and support. More often than not, however, they turn to friends rather than to campus ministers, spiritual directors, confessors, and other standard representatives of the Church. In too many instances, when they turn to formal ecclesiastical resources, they experience judgment rather than understanding. Many priests feel themselves caught in the middle, between the official teachings of the Church—on homosexuality, let us say, or masturbation, or premarital sex—and the actual experience and situation of the young Catholic who comes to them for advice and direction. Priests who lack confidence in their own good pastoral judgment tend to give the "party line" and nothing else, and that turns off the young person who concludes that the Church doesn't understand, or that he or she has no place in the Church. On the other hand, there are also priests who are so kind and pastorally sensitive that they tend to undervalue the wisdom of the Church's official tradition. Fortunately, there are still many priests and other counselors in the Church who effectively balance the two. For such priests and counselors the relationship with the young Catholic can be open and honest—and both qualities are absolutely essential for the building of trust, which is, in turn, absolutely essential for any true growth.

There is no magic formula that I am aware of for reaching disaffected or alienated youth. But without openness and honesty on the part of those representing the Church—and that includes parents as well as clergy—there is no realistic hope of reaching the young.

Q. 80. Despite all of my rationalizations, I'm having trouble communicating with my teenagers on why they should attend and participate in Mass. Got any good ideas on how I can encourage them?

I am almost tempted to say, "See above." But you've asked a more particular question than the previous person asked. You're concerned specifically with the Mass and with the challenge of encouraging your teenage children to attend Mass with you and your spouse.

You already know what *doesn't* work: threats, bribes, manipulation, guilt-trips, temper tantrums, theological arguments, and the like. When all else fails, as the saying goes, read the directions. That means doing the less exciting work of actually sitting down and trying to figure out how a thing works before plugging it in and playing the game of trial-and-error. In this case, reading the directions means sitting down with your son or daughter and asking him or her what there is about the Mass and the experience of attending Mass that he or she finds so unattractive. When you do this, you must scrupulously observe one major rule: no interruptions, no instant rebuttals, no definitive rulings from the parental bench. Take as your model the approach the Archbishop of Milwaukee, Rembert Weakland, took several years ago when he held at least six different meetings in various parts of his archdiocese to listen—really listen—to Catholic women, representing a variety of backgrounds and viewpoints, on the delicate and controversial subject of abortion. You'll be criticized for it, as he was, possibly even by your own spouse, for failing to exercise your responsibility as a parent to tell your child the difference between right and wrong. But do it anyway.

What you'll hear from your teenagers will be a variety of reasons for not attending Mass. Some will be purely self-serving, not well thought out. Others, however, will be similar to those which even you will have to admit possess a ring of truth. They may, for example, refer to the service as empty, without feeling, without any obvious commitment to what they're supposed to be doing together as a faith-community. They may be put off by the personalities and styles of the priest or priests of the parish, their lack of any apparent empathy for young people or even recognition that they exist. It is highly likely that they will be critical of the homilies given at Mass, how out of touch they are, or how narrow-minded and reactionary their view of the Church and society generally are. To be sure, a teenage son will have a different set of grievances from a teenage daughter. Your daughter may share the sense of disaffection, or outright alienation, that many Catholic women, of all ages, feel toward the institutional Church—all the way from resentment for all the time it took to approve altar girls to the continued resistance to gender-inclusive language and the ordination of women as priests. Teenage sons will have a more difficult time expressing their genuinely spiritual frustrations, but time and patience may eventually draw them out.

After listening to your teenagers, you will have every right to ask them, in turn, to hear you out, both positively and negatively. Not for the sake of point-by-point rebuttal, but rather to share your own love for the Church as well as your own personal frustrations with some church practices. They may be at once surprised and edified by your openness and your honesty. Both of these qualities are rare enough today that their appearance always draws a crowd, so to speak. You will have their attention, I guarantee it. And perhaps both parent and teenage child will grow through the experience. Who knows what the Holy Spirit can accomplish when our hearts and minds are truly open to the Spirit's presence and activity?

But if the process doesn't seem to work, that's not an excuse for giving up. Patience means patience. Not just for a day, or a week, or a month, but possibly for several months, even years. Over the long haul, the most effective argument is example, or witnessing. Your teenage children will be drawn to the Eucharist if they see that it really makes a difference in *your* life, that you're not just going through the motions as a Catholic, that your Christian faith and your membership in the Church have a profoundly positive impact on your self-esteem, on your relationships with others, on your work, and most immediately on your family life. And if even *that* doesn't work, the rule is still: Patience. After all, isn't that the rule God follows in dealing with each of us? We must *all* look like teenagers in God's sight!

Q. 81. I am deeply troubled, not only by the missing youth mentioned by the previous questioner, but also by the minority of men and the presence of very few people of color. Is this really the Church? You say it is not. Which reality are we to believe?

Although the Catholic Church has grown enormously in Africa during the course of the twentieth century and although fully one-quarter of all Catholics in the United States are Hispanic, we are still largely a white, Caucasian church. In most parishes throughout the United States,

Canada, Australia, Ireland, New Zealand, and England, for example, one doesn't find more than a handful of people of color in the congregation. Of the nearly 60 million Catholics in the United States in the mid-1990s, only 2.5 million are African American. Most people of color in the United States have found their spiritual homes in predominantly black or African-American Protestant denominations, and many of those have drifted away from Christianity (the religion, they say, of their former slaveholders) into Islam. It used to be said, in fact, that the most segregated hour in the United States is between 11 o'clock and noon on Sunday when most churches hold their main worship service. If there has been some improvement in the meantime, it's not all that noticeable.

This is not a minor matter, by any means. The Church is supposed to be the human family in microcosm. It should reflect the full sweep of human diversity: cultural, racial, ethnic, economic, demographic. When it has only a "plain vanilla" look and taste to it, its function as the universal sacrament of salvation is blunted. It takes on some of the characteristics of an all-white country club—the very antithesis of what the Body of Christ is and is called to be. How the Catholic Church can more effectively reach out to people of color, especially those in the African-American community, is a matter of some pastoral complexity. What we need to do perhaps is to follow the same approach I recommended in our outreach to disaffected and uninvolved teenagers. Ask, then listen. And speak only after we have really listened, non-judgmentally. We may not like what we hear—about the dominance of white clergy and white bishops, about liturgies and preaching that are too staid and uptight, about obligatory celibacy, and about institutional racism. But more has to be done than has been done. The sacramentality of the Body of Christ—or at least of the Catholic portion thereof—is at stake.

Regarding the preponderance of women over men in the most active ranks of parishioners and diocesan workers: This is a fact that cannot be denied. Recent studies have shown that fully 80 percent or more of lay ministers at parish and diocesan levels are women, which makes the current alienation of many women from the institutional Church a matter of grave practical consequence. The Catholic Church simply cannot meet its present and future ministerial needs and responsibilities without the active involvement of Catholic women. Whether and how the present distribution of female-to-male members in ministry can or will change is another question entirely—for which there is no easy answer. There are too many factors to be considered: the psychology of men and women, the sociology of work and its attraction for and impact upon men and women, the economics of church employment as a second-income job where wages and benefits are almost always too low to support a spouse and children, the recent history of the Catholic Church in North America and elsewhere, the varieties of ministry available to women and to men, e.g., some for nurturing, others for leadership.

One of the reasons, rarely spoken in public, that some Catholics have offered in opposition to women's ordination is that religion, by its very nature, is a women's enterprise. By excluding women from positions of pastoral leadership, the Catholic Church maintains a kind of ecological balance which insures that the Church will not become totally feminized. While not a valid argument against women's ordination, it should make us think more deeply about the question you raise: why is church activity, below the level of pastoral leadership, more attractive to women than to men?

Q. 82. Most Catholic gatherings, at least in the United States, are not only white and predominantly female in composition, but they also tend to be drawn from the ranks of the economically well-off. Aren't we in danger of becoming an elitist Church and a contradiction of Jesus' central concern for the poor?

If I were to judge solely on the basis of my own limited experience as a speaker before Catholic audiences in every part of the United States and Canada, I would have to agree with your observation about the predominance of white females at such gatherings. And I have tried to reflect on that phenomenon in my previous answers. It's more difficult, however, to make a judgment about the economic status of such audiences. I suppose it would be safe to conclude that few of the very poor, the so-called underclass, are represented at such gatherings. But it's not because the Church doesn't have many members from that economic level. It's more likely that they either can't afford the time and money to attend such meetings, or they are simply not connected with the network of Catholics who arrange and participate in them. The suggestion that Catholics who do attend are from the upper-middle class or higher is more dubious. That is not my impression. On the contrary, many are employees of the Church, whether as ministers, staff personnel, or volunteers. Few are likely to have appreciably increased their net worth through such employment.

However, these observations do not in any way refute your concern about the image of the Church and about its not losing sight of its abiding commitment to the poor and the marginalized. As Catholics in First World countries ascend the economic ladder, there is a constant danger that the social, economic, and political views of their new peer-groups will become more decisive in their thinking and behavior than the values of the Gospel itself, and particularly the teaching and example of Jesus himself.

Jesus' own earthly origins were rooted in poverty (Luke 1:52-53; 2:7,24). In Luke's version of the Sermon on the Mount, Jesus first blesses the poor, assuring them that the Reign of God is theirs (6:20). In the Parable of the Rich Man and Lazarus (16:19-31), to which Pope John Paul II has appealed so frequently, Jesus reserves his special wrath for the indifference and hard-heartedness of the rich man in the face of Lazarus' abject poverty.

Scripture scholars point out that what is of major, if not revolutionary, significance in Jesus' attitude toward the poor is that the poor should have any place at all in the divine scheme of things. In contradiction to traditional thinking on poverty, even within Judaism itself, Jesus taught that being poor is no obstacle to one's entrance into the Kingdom of God. On the contrary, if there is any economically-based obstacle at all, it is wealth, not poverty. "But woe to you who are rich, for you have received your consolation" (Luke 6:24). Indeed, he also said, "it is easier for a camel to go through the eye of a needle than for someone who is rich to enter the kingdom of God" (Matt 19:24).

Modern Catholic social teaching reinforces the teaching of Jesus, especially with its emphasis on the "preferential option for the poor." "The Church's love for the poor," Pope John Paul II wrote in his 1991 encyclical *Centesimus Annus*, "which is essential for [the Church] and a part of its constant tradition, impels it to give attention to a world in which poverty is threatening to assume massive proportions in spite of technological and economic progress....[L]ove for the poor...is made concrete in the promotion of justice" (nn. 57,58). Rich, poor, or middle class, the real mark of the Body of Christ is its passion for and practice of justice.

Q. 83. Why is liberation theology perceived as a threat by some in the Church establishment?

Liberation theology, which first appeared in Latin America in the late 1960s, under the impact particularly of the Second Vatican Council's Pastoral Constitution on the Church in the Modern World (1965) and Pope Paul VI's powerful social encyclical, *Populorum Progressio* (1967), was never intended as a threat to the Church establishment. It was simply a new way of doing theology, based on the recognition that one's understanding of the faith and of its application to our lives is determined in largest part by who is doing the theology, where it is done, and with whom the theologian lives and works. Since the Gospel is a message of liberation from oppression of every kind— economic, social, political, cultural, historical, and moral—we can only reflect on and interpret that Gospel in solidarity with the poor and the oppressed. One must "do" the truth before one can really "see" it. The fancy Greek word for such a method is *praxis*.

Liberation theologians rejected the conventional notions that poverty and suffering are God's will and should be accepted as such, and that charity, not social justice, is the proper response to poverty and suffering. On the contrary, poverty and oppression are evils to be overcome. Since they are systemic as well as individual in character, they must be addressed institutionally as well as personally. Structures must be changed, not just hearts.

But changing structures is the task of politicians, not theologians. What liberation theologians are called upon to do is prophetic criticism. They are to unmask the false ideas (known as ideologies) embodied in oppressive systems that support economic, social, and political privilege at the expense of the poor and the disenfranchised. Eventually—perhaps inevitably—the method of prophetic criticism was applied to the institutional Church itself. The hierarchy was compared with the political and economic elites in secular society. The hierarchy's resistance to reform and to the sharing of power was said to parallel that of the secular elites.

The Vatican issued a critique of liberation theology in 1984, noting an "insufficiently critical" borrowing of Marxist concepts, such as the class struggle, and warning of the danger of reducing faith to politics. It also criticized liberation theology's emphasis on institutional, or systemic, sin, at the expense of individual and personal sin, and its undermining of the Church's authority by identifying the hierarchy with a privileged class. One liberation theologian, Leonardo Boff, a Brazilian, was explicitly censured for making that last argument. In 1986, however, Pope John Paul II, in a letter to the Brazilian bishops, referred to the "useful and necessary" character of liberation theology.

Perhaps the most powerful endorsement of the essential aims of liberation theology—in addition to the encyclical *Populorum Progressio*—came in Pope Paul VI's 1975 apostolic exhortation, *Evangelii Nuntiandi* (On Evangelization in the Modern World): "But evangelization would not be complete if it did not take account of the unceasing interplay of the Gospel and of humanity's concrete life, both personal and social. This is why evangelization involves an explicit message...about the rights and duties of every human being,...about life in society, about international life, peace, justice, and development—a message especially energetic today about liberation" (n. 29).

Q. 84. Are Catholic schools the best vehicle for formal education in our faith?

I suppose it depends on what you mean by "schools." If you mean parochial schools only, then the answer is, "Not necessarily." A good parish-based religious education program can be as effective, and sometimes even a more effective vehicle than a parish school. There are many variable factors, one of which is the actual commitment of the school to religious education as reflected in the professional preparation and continuing education of its religion teachers, the quality of the textbooks and other resources, the environment provided for learning, and the linkage with the wider pastoral life of the faith-community. But just as there are excellent, good, mediocre, and poor parochial schools, so there are excellent-to-poor religious education programs. One must take it on a case-by-case basis.

Whether schooling as such is an important contributor to formal education in the faith is a larger and different question. I would suggest, on the basis of the Church's own historical experience, that schooling—at all levels—has been, and continues to be, a crucial and almost indispensable means of educating younger Catholics in the faith. This is so because schooling involves much more than the transmission of knowledge. It provides a stable environment for learning, an environment that is communal in character. Father Andrew Greeley, one of America's strongest advocates of Catholic schools, argues that it is the "community-forming" component of Catholic schools that explains their ultimate effectiveness.

But notice I said, "at all levels." The level of which I am most familiar is that of the university. The President Emeritus of the University of Notre Dame, Father Theodore Hesburgh, C.S.C., is fond of saying that a Catholic university is "the place where the Church does its thinking." By no means is it the only place, but it is a special and unique place. Where else can the faith be subjected to the kind of intense, critical, thoroughgoing analysis and review as one finds in a Catholic college or university department of theology? The result is not the weakening of faith, but its strengthening. Faith, like a human person, is always strengthened when it sheds excess weight—the excess weight of superstition, pious assumptions, and outright error. Given the present environment in the Church, Catholic universities and colleges are the only places where this theological exercise program can be conducted without interference from those who fear that it is more likely to kill the patient than make the patient healthier.

Formal schooling in the faith also takes place in seminaries, high schools, and parochial schools. Is any one of these the "best" vehicle for formal education in the faith. Who can say? What is important is that the Church employ all the vehicles it has to the fullest, because the task of education in faith is at once urgent and challenging.

Q. 85. How can we help parents realize that they are the first and foremost educators of their children?

No one is better equipped to answer that question than parish ministers—almost always lay women—who are directly involved in the important work of sacramental preparation of the young. They are intimately familiar with the possibilities as well as the frustrations of the task. It is they who have the exhilarating experience of seeing parents come to life, as it were, and not only begin to take responsibility for their children's education and formation in the faith, but to do so with enthusiasm and pride. But it is they, too, who have the often depressing experience of sensing the impatience and even hostility of parents, resentful of the fact that they have somehow been "dragged into" a process that the sisters or the lay ministers should be taking care of for them. No amount of intellectual argument—appeals to Scripture or to the teachings of the Church—will make any difference to them, because their problem isn't intellectual. It goes deeper than that. Call it insecurity, if you will. These are adult Catholics who know in their hearts—notwithstanding their occasional spurts of theological bravado—that their own intellectual grasp of the faith is tenuous at best. They may not admit it even to themselves, and certainly not to "that woman" in charge of sacramental preparation, but they lack confidence in their ability to do the job. And so they lash out at those who would have them try.

Our pastoral challenge, therefore, is not to see how much theology and church directives we can cram into the heads of parents, but to establish an environment and an atmosphere in which parents can feel more at ease about the responsibility being placed before them. They must be helped to realize, for example, that others are in the same boat, that the woman or man sitting next to them is probably no better prepared than they think themselves to be—and may even share many of the same anxieties about the matter. In other words, one starts slowly, works patiently, and builds at least a modicum of community. From there it is at least possible, perhaps even probable, that many, if not most, in the group will begin to change in their attitude and outlook. There will always be a few stubborn holdouts, but their resistance should not unduly discourage us nor paralyze the entire process of education and formation.

When the more open-minded are ready for something a bit more "intellectual," we can point out that in Catholic teaching the family is the most basic unit in society, more basic even than the Church. In recent years, in fact, the family has been referred to, by the Second Vatican Council and by modern popes, as a "domestic church." It is the place where the Gospel is first proclaimed, in word and by example. Where the symbols of faith, like the sign of the cross, are first transmitted. Where Christian community is first experienced. A parish is no better or no worse than the families which make it up, and a diocese is no better or no worse than the parishes that make *it* up, and the universal Church is no better or no worse than the dioceses that make it up. Which brings us back once again to the family, and especially to the parents, who are indeed the first and foremost educators in the faith.

Q. 86. As a medical scientist I am deeply concerned about the education of our Church's hierarchy concerning the moral issues resulting from the rapid advances in the biological sciences. How do you envision the most effective way for our Church leaders and teachers to incorporate these advances into their teaching for the next century?

The hierarchy is no different from the rest of us. The way you learn about something you don't know anything about is by seeking the help and guidance of people who *do* know something about it. It may be a matter of reading up on a subject, taking a course, or engaging in a kind of private tutorial with an expert. But knowledge doesn't come through direct inspiration or by a process of osmosis. You have to admit your ignorance and be willing to take the steps to correct it. That requires a certain measure of self-knowledge, honesty, and discipline. Not everyone has those qualities. Without them, however, growth in knowledge is impossible.

In the case of the rapid growth in the biological sciences and the almost exponential growth in medical and bioethical issues, there is no easy substitute for the educative process I've just described. But add to it the importance, and inestimable value, of direct contact with practitioners in the medical facilities themselves: scientists, physicians, surgeons, hospital administrators, laboratory technicians, and the like.

Fortunately, those of us in the United States have a particular advantage. We have both the most highly advanced and sophisticated medical technology available in the entire world, and also the leading medical ethicists and bioethicists in the Church. There is no reasonable excuse, therefore, for any of us—Church leader or teacher—to plead ignorance about these serious moral issues, to speak out on them without proper preparation, or to assume that one already knows enough about the subject.

The field of bioethics, after all, emerged as a distinct area of moral inquiry only as recently as the late 1960s and early 1970s. The development was prompted by such new procedures as heart transplants, genetic experimentation, in vitro fertilization, new definitions of death, and the withdrawal of life-sustaining treatment. These were complicated by the fact that the new medical technology came at a very high price. Questions arose about the ethical validity of withholding exceedingly costly medical procedures—bone marrow transplants and various forms of dialysis, for example—from some but not from others. There were also legal complications. Lawsuits were initiated to prevent doctors from withdrawing life-support systems from comatose patients. The practice of physician-assisted suicides raised questions of criminal responsibility. And so forth.

The more complicated the issues, the more imperative it is for all of us to learn from "the best and the brightest" in the field, and not simply to rely on traditional answers to relatively simple questions that have long since been rendered out-of-date by the rapid growth in medical technology and practice.

Q. 87. Do you believe that the Holy Spirit is working in our Church today through the rising charismatic church? If so, how will this change the Church?

One can never be sure whether and where the Holy Spirit is at work in the Church. One can only make judgments based on observations. But those judgments are always fallible. Many times they serve primarily to reinforce views already held. Thus, Catholics who are generally happy with the changes wrought by the Second Vatican Council have no difficulty whatever in hearing the council referred to by popes and others as the work of the Spirit. Catholics who have been more troubled by postconciliar developments are less likely to use that language. Catholics who favor the ordination of women to the priesthood regard the growing support for it as an effect of the Holy Spirit. Catholics who oppose the ordination of women would clearly not agree. And the same is the case with the charismatic movement itself—a movement based on the assumption that we are living in a new age of the Holy Spirit and that charismatic Catholics are harbingers of the Church to come. Catholics who are active participants in the charismatic movement find it very easy, even imperative, to credit the Holy Spirit with its rise and continued existence. Catholics who are less enamored of the movement are reluctant to make that connection.

Even apart from the movement known as the Catholic Charismatic Renewal, one must affirm the presence of charisms, or gifts of the Holy Spirit, from the very earliest days of the Church. These charisms included the gifts of wisdom, knowledge, healing, prophecy, tongues, and interpretation (1 Cor 12:4-11). There was a debate at Vatican II, however, on whether the age of charisms had ceased. More conservative bishops insisted that it had, while more progressive bishops, like Belgium's Cardinal Leo-Josef Suenens, disagreed. The latter view won out. The council's Dogmatic Constitution on the Church declared that the Holy Spirit also "sanctifies and leads the People of God" apart from the sacraments. Charisms are "activated by one and the same Spirit, who allots to each individually just as the Spirit chooses" (1 Cor 12:11). In one of the most important of all the conciliar statements, the Constitution insisted that the Spirit "distributes special graces among the faithful of every rank" (n. 12). The statement is important because of its immediately practical consequences. If the Spirit does indeed distribute charisms "among the faithful of every rank," one cannot argue that every apparent conflict between the Church's official teachers and the Church's rank-and-file membership is always to be resolved in favor of the teachers because they, unlike the rest, are guided by the Holy Spirit. The Spirit guides the whole Church, including "the faithful of every rank." Not every apparent conflict between official teachers and the faithful of other ranks, therefore, can be resolved automatically in favor of the magisterium. One has to look more deeply and more prayerfully into the matter.

Unfortunately, some elements in the Catholic charismatic movement have lapsed into a more rigid, institutionalized approach. In fact, it is difficult to see how, in their view, the council's teaching on the "democratization" of the Spirit's charisms has any practical meaning. In the final accounting, it seems that the charisms are reserved exclusively to the faithful of certain ranks, namely, those of the hierarchy.

How can the charismatic movement change the Church at large? The impact of the charismatic movement as such may be limited, but the teaching of Vatican II on the universal distribution of charisms is not. In fact, it has already had a profound effect on the Catholic Church: in its theology, its preaching, and its ordinary pastoral practice. The institutional aspects of Catholicism are still very much a part of its life and thinking, but since the council there is a much greater appreciation for the charismatic dimension of the Church, which means a greater openness to change and to diversity, and to the freedom that makes both possible.

Q. 88. How can we deal with factions in the Church today?

The best way to deal with factions in the Church is the same way that James Madison, in *The Federalist Papers* (no. 10), prescribed for dealing with religious factions in the young American Republic: encourage a multiplicity of religious bodies, and don't allow any one of them to gain an unfair advantage over all others. Madison defined a faction as "a number of citizens, whether amounting to a majority or a minority of the whole, who are united and actuated by some common impulse of passion, or of interest, adverse to the rights of other citizens, or to the permanent and aggregate interests of the community."

Factions have been part of the Church from the very beginning. As many as four different parties existed in Corinth, when Paul sent his first Letter. "Now I appeal to you, brothers and sisters," he wrote, "by the name of our Lord Jesus Christ, that all of you be in agreement and that there be no divisions among you, but that you be united in the same mind and the same purpose. For it has been reported to me by Chloe's people that there are quarrels among you, my brothers and sisters. What I mean is that each of you says, 'I belong to Paul,' or 'I belong to Apollos,' or 'I belong to Cephas,' or 'I belong to Christ.' Has Christ been divided?" (1 Cor 1:10-13). New Testament scholars also remind us of the deep and bitter divisions within the communities associated with the Beloved Disciple, John, the Evangelist of communal love.

So it should not surprise us that Catholics, who have been baptized into the same Christ and who profess the same faith and who partake of the same Eucharist, have been in conflict with one another down through the centuries, even into our own time. That doesn't make it acceptable, of course. Such conflict, and the factionalism that foments it, is corrosive of the life of the Church, which is called to be a sacrament of the unity for which Christ prayed at the Last Supper. But on this side of the Second Coming of Christ it is impossible to immunize the Church from conflict and factionalism. As long as the Church is composed of frail and imperfect human beings, it will always bear within itself the effects of Original Sin.

How, then, can we best deal with the inevitable? By doing what Madison suggests, that is, by encouraging as much diversity and free expression of ideas in the Church, by seeing to it that many flowers bloom in the Church's garden, and by taking care lest "a bruised reed" be broken or "a smoldering wick" be quenched (Matt 12:20). It means treating one another with respect, however vigorously we disagree, and defending others' rights to express their faith in ways consistent with their own conscience, without harm to the common good of the Church itself. In a word, it means living as Christians are supposed to live.

Q. 89. How can we bring the extremes of The Wanderer and the National Catholic Reporter crowds together, or is there no hope of this?

This is really a spin-off of the previous question about factionalism in the Church. The same principles and points apply here as well. However, I would not be inclined to agree with the underlying premise of the question, namely, that the *National Catholic Reporter* is as far to the left as *The Wanderer* is to the right. The *NCR* is highly critical of certain members of the hierarchy, does in-depth reports on problems in dioceses and other religious institutions, exposes ecclesiastical events and initiatives that were intended to remain secret and, therefore, beyond public scrutiny and criticism, and makes available a breadth of opinion in the Church that would otherwise be denied a Catholic forum. For some, this makes the *NCR* a wildly liberal or even radical paper. It is not. The *NCR* simply validates Pope Pius XII's argument back in the 1950s that public opinion is an essential element in the Church. Without it, the Church's leaders do not have access to all the necessary information they need before making important pastoral decisions.

The Wanderer also has a valid role to play in the Catholic Church. Its voice, however strident some may think it becomes on occasion, deserves to be heard and its arguments and complaints merit attention and response. But it is difficult to see how an objective comparison of the two papers could lead one to conclude that there is no real difference in their respective styles of reporting and editorializing. The *NCR* may be strongly critical of a Vatican policy or of an individual bishop's administration of his diocese, for example, but to my knowledge it has never questioned the authentic Catholic faith of those whom it criticizes. That is not the case with *The Wanderer*. Too often, its reports go far beyond a critical analysis of another's words and actions—to the extreme, even rash, judgment that the individual under review is really a heretic and an enemy of the Church.

Whatever one thinks of either paper, we are all bound—liberal, conservative, and moderate centrist alike—by the same virtues of love and justice. It is a violation of Christ's love to ridicule a sister or brother in the Body of Christ simply because we do not agree with their theology or their spirituality or their pastoral opinions, and it is a violation of justice to trash the name and reputation of another. Whether done by a liberal, a conservative, or a moderate centrist, it is wrong.

The most effective way to deal with the corrosive effects of factionalism in the Church, as I suggested in the previous answer, is by practicing the Gospel, by truly living the faith that we all verbally profess.

Q. 90. Do you think that in the future the Church will welcome back into the community divorced Catholics who have remarried outside the Church?

Yes, I do. In fact, it is already happening in many parishes. Catholics who are known to be involved in second marriages without benefit of canonical dissolution of the first marriage are accepted at the

Communion table and perform various ministerial functions in service to the whole parish. I hasten to add that this is not in accord with the current discipline of the Catholic Church. On the contrary, when three German bishops—one the president of the national episcopal conference and another a distinguished theologian—urged a review of the current policy toward divorced-and-remarried Catholics in 1994, the Vatican rejected their proposal and reaffirmed the policy.

But the incidence of divorce and remarriage is not going to disappear in the next century, as unfortunate as that may be. It is simply a sad fact of life that many marriages—in some countries at least fifty percent—do not survive the often severe pressures inherent in human relationships. When those involved in divorce are still relatively young, as many are, it is also unrealistic to suppose that most of them will remain celibate for the remainder of their lives. Given our extended life-expectancy, that could mean more than fifty years. In any case, many divorced Catholics do in fact remarry and many of those second marriages prove to be stable, unlike the first. What is the Church to do in the face of this pastoral reality? How is the Church to deal pastorally with so many members of its flock who are in canonically irregular marriages and yet who show every sign of an authentic Christian faith and a vocation to Christian discipleship within the faith-community? Are all of them to be excluded definitively and for the rest of their lives from the Communion table? Are their ministerial gifts to be denied? Are they to be treated as second-class citizens in the Body of Christ? The German bishops, on pastoral grounds alone, concluded that the current policy cannot deal effectively with this situation. The Vatican disagreed.

Your question did not ask if I support the current official policy of the Catholic Church toward the divorced-and-remarried. You asked only what I foresee in the future regarding a possible change in the Church's pastoral approach. I think there will be such a change.

Q. 91. How far into the 21st century do you see/predict the rule of celibacy becoming a matter of choice for priests and religious?

You are, of course, referring to the discipline of obligatory celibacy currently in force in the Roman Catholic Church, that is, the Latin rite. (I have already given the historical background for this discipline in *Q. 57*, above.) Celibacy is not required of priests (although it is required of bishops) in the various Eastern-rite Catholic churches. But neither is it universally imposed even in the Latin rite. In recent years several former Episcopal priests who are married have been received into the Catholic Church and been reordained conditionally as Catholic diocesan priests. They have not been required to separate themselves from their wives, nor have they been required to live as brother and sister. So we already have a married priesthood today, even in the Roman Catholic Church. The question, therefore, is not when will we have a married diocesan clergy in the Roman Catholic Church, but when will *all* Roman Catholic diocesan priests have the same freedom to marry as these former Episcopal priests enjoy?

Celibacy for religious is another matter, however. Priests in religious orders and congregations also take vows of poverty, chastity, and obedience. They commit themselves, in principle at least, to life in community, with all that community life implies: common worship and prayer, common table, common property, obedience to religious superiors, and in some cases stability of residence. Celibacy has a different meaning and purpose in the context of a vowed life lived in community, although it is entirely conceivable that in the future there will be religious communities of married as well as of unmarried members. There is no absolute antithesis between the married state and life in religious community, although history yields little precedent for it thus far.

Many questions about the future are difficult, if not totally impossible, to answer. One is reduced to following hunches or making rather wild guesses. But the celibacy question is not so difficult to answer. I am convinced that it's not *whether* obligatory celibacy will end for *all* Roman Catholic diocesan priests, but *when*.

Q. 92. Will future priests still be "professional clergy," set apart and trained? Or do you think that we'll ever "raise and acclaim" regular parishioners, who will then be ordained to officiate at the Eucharist?

If you are asking whether the commitment to priestly ministry in the future will be temporary rather than permanent, my answer is, "Yes and no." Yes, we will probably have instances, perhaps many, of temporary engagements in priestly ministry that could be either full-time or part-time for the duration of the service. But I cannot imagine a time when the Church will not require a large cadre of ordained priests who are theologically educated, professionally trained, and spiritually formed for priestly ministry, so crucial is this ministry for the everyday life and mission of the Church. Given the Church's and the individual's investment in such a preparation, a temporary commitment to priestly ministry (five or ten years, perhaps?) would be wholly impractical, in my judgment, particularly if it became the rule rather than the exception.

But this is not to deny your implied hope that the call to the priesthood in the future will be more a matter of response to the invitation of the faith-community than of the candidate's personal choice, or self-selection. If that should prove to be the case, as I expect it will, the change will not be without precedent. On the contrary, that is how vocations were determined in the early Church, and especially for bishops, including the Bishop of Rome, the pope. The community recognized the existence of the necessary gifts in a particular individual and then invited him—sometimes even importuned him—to accept its call to priestly ministry and later to episcopal ministry.

As the division between clergy and laity widened, especially after the conversion of the Emperor Constantine in the early fourth century when clergy became civil officials with all the rights and privileges attached thereto, the laity were progressively excluded from decision-making in the Church, just as they were increasingly excluded from direct and active participation in the liturgy. The governance and ministries of the Church became a clerical affair. Vocations, then, were determined not by the community but by the bishop and his immediate advisers. Candidates for the priesthood were trained in bishops' houses and presented to the community for ordination when the bishop deemed them ready. By the time of the Protestant Reformation, however, it was painfully obvious that priests were woefully unprepared for the responsibilities of ministry and pastoral leadership. Many laity were better educated than the clergy.

Perhaps the most significant reform undertaken by the Council of Trent in the mid-sixteenth century was the establishment of seminaries for the education and spiritual formation of priests. The vocation to priesthood was now determined not by the bishop alone, but by the bishop in consultation with his seminary faculty and staff. This system continues to function even today, with only a few modifications since the Second Vatican Council. The first is the broadening of seminary faculties, staffs, and admissions boards to include non-clergy—and women especially. The second is the introduction of the deacon-year of pastoral service outside the seminary. Those with whom the transitional deacon serves in a parish are invited to be present at the ordination ceremony and to testify publicly to the deacon's readiness for priestly ministry. The third is the ceremonial applause from the congregation when invited by the ordaining bishop to express its approval for the ordination that is about to take place. But none of these changes goes far enough to insure that a vocation to the ordained priesthood will genuinely be determined by the faith-communities the priest is expected to serve. A priestly vocation is still a matter of self-selection. A candidate decides on his own, perhaps with the assistance of a spiritual director, that he "wants to be a priest." It is almost never the case that a young man, already active in some parish ministry, is recognized and then strongly encouraged by a significant number of similarly active parishioners as a person clearly equipped with the personal gifts needed for effective priestly ministry. In most cases, the candidate's fellow parishioners don't even know him, except perhaps by sight. And in too many cases, those who *do* know him are not heartened by the news of his interest in the priesthood. Until celibacy and priestly ministry are separated once and for all, these instances are likely to continue to occur.

I do believe that, when obligatory celibacy and the exclusion of women are no longer a part of the Roman Catholic Church's discipline concerning the ordained priesthood, the practice of self-selection will subside and the active involvement of the community in the call to priesthood will increase.

Q. 93. How do we realistically say we will remain a eucharistic community with (1) the strong possibility that the ordained priesthood will remain solely male for many years to come, (2) the lack of participation in the Eucharist by parents of children/teens, (3) poorly led Eucharists by many of the present clergy, and (4) more conservative leadership from the bishops?

First, what do we mean by a eucharistic community? It is a faith-community which is centered on the Eucharist as the "summit" and the "source" of its entire Christian life, to use the words of the Second Vatican Council's Constitution on the Sacred Liturgy (n. 10). A eucharistic community's faith is nourished and sustained by the Word of God that is proclaimed, by the Gospel that is preached, by the body and blood of Christ that it offers to God in thanksgiving and that it feeds upon, and by the sisterly and brotherly communion that it experiences through this sharing in Holy Communion. A eucharistic community is one that is gathered out of the world (which is the root meaning of the word "church") and then dismissed ("Go, the Mass is ended") for service to others *in* the world. So long as the Church can still do all that is included in the reality of the Eucharist, it will remain a eucharistic community. Whether the presiding minister, or celebrant, is male or female, married or unmarried, effective or ineffective, is accidental to the Eucharist and to the nature of the Church as a eucharistic community. And so, too, are the numbers and categories of active participants. And so, too, finally, is the theological and pastoral orientation of the hierarchy, whether it be liberal, or conservative, or safely moderate.

Now, this is not to deny any of the four concerns expressed in your question. Let me address them, point by point:

(1) I have already shared with you my prediction that celibacy will become optional for *all* Roman Catholic priests sometime in the next century, more likely sooner than later, given the growing vocations crisis. I agree that it would enhance the celebration of the Eucharist if presiders were drawn from a wider, more representative segment of the Church than is currently the case.

(2) I'm not sure what to make of your second concern. Most observers report that Catholic adults are more likely to return to the liturgical practice of their faith once they have married and begun to raise a family. They attend Mass "for the sake of the children." What you're probably suggesting is that they are only bodily present, and that this is the case because their return has not been prompted by a reenergizing of faith but by a more sociologically-based concern for their children's upbringing with a set of religious values and traditions. If that's your point, it's well taken.

(3) One cannot deny the problem of poorly led eucharistic cele-

brations—which are "celebrations" in name only. Too many priests lack the necessary personal skills and natural qualities to truly lead a diverse faith-community in worship. In some few cases, no doubt, there is even a lack of deeply rooted faith in what the Eucharist is all about. They "recite" prayers and go through the motions as if by rote, without feeling, without apparent conviction. And that shows. The solution is to attract a higher type of candidate to the priesthood, and to demand that a demonstrated capacity for liturgical presence and leadership, not to say also preaching, be an essential requirement for ordination.

(4) The theological and pastoral orientation of the hierarchy tends to change with each new pontificate, particularly in the case of relatively lengthy pontificates (over ten years). During the 15-year pontificate of Paul VI a fairly broad variety of priests were named bishops. In the United States, for example, the Apostolic Delegate, Archbishop Jean Jadot, took great care and pride in selecting pastorally-oriented bishops. During the even lengthier pontificate of John Paul II, bishops all over the world have been selected on a different basis. Given the pope's expressed concerns about some highly public developments in the postconciliar Church, bishops had to be unquestionably loyal to the directives of the Holy See, particularly on matters pertaining to sexual ethics (e.g., birth control, sterilization, in vitro fertilization, abortion) and the ordained priesthood (e.g., obligatory celibacy, women's ordination). In the absence of such institutional loyalty, even evidence of a great capacity for pastoral leadership was insufficient grounds for appointment. As I said, however, pontificates inevitably change, and so, too, do the types of bishops named.

Q. 94. What can we who work in the parish do to facilitate the change or shift of the Church into the 21st century? What obstacles do you see? What present reality contributes to this shift? What are you hopeful about?

The first and most important thing you can do is to perform your various ministries in the most effective, dedicated way possible. There is much truth in the old saying, "Nothing succeeds like success." If we really practice what we preach and teach about the Gospel, about the nature of ministry, about the need for a caring and just Church, the parish is going to sit up and take notice. And perhaps the diocese as well. It is also the most telling form of criticism of those who do not measure up to their own ministerial responsibilities, including members of the clergy. Ordinary parishioners may not be able to identify, much less tell the difference between the theology of Karl Rahner and that of Hans Urs von Balthasar, or between *America* magazine and *First Things*, or between Pax Christi and Opus Dei, but they *can* tell the difference between good ministry and poor ministry, between healthy, well-balanced, and open-minded ministers who really care about those they serve, and defensive, insecure, and rigid ministers who are more interested in preserving and protecting the prerogatives of their office. Those ordinary parishioners will choose the healthy over the unhealthy every time, because their own human and Christian instincts are sound. And they're thinking not only of themselves, but especially of their children.

The obstacles to which you refer are posed by those who feel themselves threatened by another's healthy exercise of ministry, especially if that ministry is being exercised by a woman, and a lay woman in particular. Although they can never admit it, probably not even to themselves, they feel diminished, even judged, by the success of others. And so they try, perhaps unwittingly or perhaps deliberately, to thwart that success by curtailing or impeding the minister's activity. It happens in a variety of ways. Job descriptions are changed and responsibilities are shifted to other, more pliant staff members. In the extreme, the "rival" minister is simply fired, regardless of her excellent job-performance reviews and the esteem she enjoys among the most active members of the parish. Sometimes, however, the obstacles come not from the clergy but from other laity, even other women, who can also feel threatened by the success of a strong, professionally skilled woman minister. But that's getting me into an area I'd prefer not to dwell upon. Women readers who have found themselves in such situations know exactly what I mean.

The "present reality" that "contributes to this shift" is a Church that is newly animated by the Holy Spirit, particularly at the Second Vatican Council. The resistance to the renewal and reforms brought about by the council is itself a testimony to the council's and the Spirit's abiding power. After all, we can only afford to ignore what seems to have no chance of success. We actively oppose what we take seriously.

Neither I nor anyone else in the Church could be hopeful about the future if we did not believe, as the 1985 Extraordinary Synod of Bishops testified, that the Second Vatican Council was truly a "work of the Holy Spirit."

Q. 95. What form do you see the Church assuming in the next century, from the worship community level to the papacy?

Predictions can be wild hunches, educated guesses, or guarded extrapolations, and sometimes a combination of all three. I prefer the last method, of extrapolation. It doesn't allow you to anticipate sudden, unprecedented lurches in one direction or another, but it is more likely to be accurate more often than the other two methods. Basically, extrapolation draws a line forward from present trends, and imagines how something might look in five, fifteen, or fifty years if those present trends continue. The method of extrapolation isn't good at determining exactly when a change might occur, but it can predict, with a fair amount of reliability, that it will eventually occur. I know of no one, for example, who predicted that the Berlin Wall would come crashing down as early as November 1989, but several shrewd observers of the world political scene knew that the old Soviet Union could not forever support its enormously expensive military establishment, given the worsening state of its economy.

When applying the method of extrapolation to the Church, therefore, one should first note the current pastoral, theological, and sociological trends and then draw from them the most likely outcomes. Among the most important trends in the Catholic Church today, promoted in large part by the reforms of the Second Vatican Council, are the following: (1) a growing recognition that the Church is not an exclusively clerical enterprise, that the laity have their own proper role in the ministries and even the governance of the Church; (2) an increased sense of responsibility in the area once known as the social apostolate, that is, in matters pertaining to social justice, human rights, and peace; (3) a gradually developing appreciation for the importance of each local church and of its special pastoral experiences and needs, with a corresponding move away from a highly centralized concept of the Church, where policies are imposed by the Vatican on everyone, regardless of local diversity; and (4) a recognition that the Church is larger than the Catholic Church, that there are other churches within the Body of Christ from whom we can learn and with whom we can work for the common cause of the Gospel.

Should trends of this sort continue, as I expect they will, we might expect the following developments:

(1) The laity will be even more directly involved in the ministerial life of the Church and in its pastoral governance. Specifically, what we find already happening in the liturgies of many progressive parishes will become an almost universal phenomenon. Laity will fill every significant liturgical role with the exception of that of presider, but the presider will as likely be married as celibate, and eventually as likely female as male. Laity will also be involved, in much the same way as they are today in the Episcopal Church, for example, in the nomination and election of bishops.

(2) The Church will continue to expand its role in the temporal order, not only in seeking governmental aid to parochial schools or in opposing funds for abortions, but also in advocating and defending the rights of society's most vulnerable members: the poor, the disabled, the elderly, the unborn, the homeless, gays and lesbians, and so forth. The most important single advance over present circumstances will be the Church's eventual recognition that justice must be practiced at home, within the Church itself, if the Church's preaching on behalf of justice is to have meaning or credibility for those outside the Church. Applying justice in the Church, however, will effect a major shift in the way the Church raises funds from its own membership.

(3) It will be almost taken for granted that very few policies and practices can be imposed upon, or applied to, every local church around the world. The Catholic Church will be an even more pluralistic community than it is today: liturgically, canonically, and ministerially. The pope will no longer personally approve the appointment of all bishops, and he himself will be elected by the World Synod of Bishops, not by the College of Cardinals.

(4) Intercommunion will become normalized between churches, at least on special occasions and feasts, and the ordained ministries of

the various churches will be mutually recognized as valid instruments of the Gospel.

Q. 96. Do you perceive the future Church you describe as coming about with those who are in power in our hierarchical structure or in spite of them? I see our own archbishop struggling to find inroads for the possibility of dialogue, but there seem to be too few signs of receptivity.

The forces that will bring about the changes I have just described are not limited to the hierarchy. In fact, hierarchies—whether religious, political, corporate, or academic—rarely, if ever, initiate revolutionary change, because revolutionary change modifies the power structure of which they are themselves a part. Of course, the principal force for change in the Church is the Holy Spirit. In the end, only the Spirit can accomplish what seems otherwise impossible to accomplish, given the natural resistance that every institution mounts against the threat of fundamental, structural change.

Another factor, also inspired in one way or another by the Holy Spirit, is the deep faith commitment and courage of many natural leaders within the ranks of the laity, clergy, and religious. Never before in the entire 2000-year history of Christianity has there been such a highly educated church membership, at all levels. With education, however, comes the capacity and the impulse to criticize received ideas and received structures and patterns of behavior. Educated people don't accept things at face-value. They ask "Why?" and "Why not?"

A third force is circumstantial. The configuration of the priesthood will change by force of circumstances, not by force of argument (even though the argument may be valid). The circumstances are such now—and will be increasingly so—that the Catholic Church simply cannot sustain an all-male, celibate priesthood for many more decades, any more than the dilapidated economy of the former Soviet Union could sustain its hugely expensive war-machine. The Soviet Union did not dissolve because Marxist ideology was suddenly found to be flawed. It dissolved because it ran out of the money necessary to pay for the military power needed to keep it together.

Popes and bishops can, if they wish, slow down the pace of

change. They can even stop it for a time. In some few instances, they can also turn it back upon itself, replacing some of the new order with some of the old. The last phenomenon is known as restorationism. But history moves forward—under the impulse of the Holy Spirit, of dedicated and committed human beings, and of social circumstances beyond anyone's control—in spite of the petty efforts of some to hold it back.

I am reminded of Pope John XXIII's opening speech at the Second Vatican Council in October of 1962. "In the present order of things," he said, "Divine Providence is leading us to a new order of human relations which, by humanity's own efforts and even beyond humanity's very expectations, are directed toward the fulfillment of God's superior and inscrutable designs. And everything, even human differences, leads to the greater good of the Church." I share John XXIII's spirit of hope.

Q. 97. As a young Catholic woman, what can I do to help the Church move toward the future? Please give some practical, everyday examples. I am hungry for change.

I was asked a variation of this question from a member of an audience at Rockhurst College in Kansas City a while back. Did I have any "strategies for survival" in today's Church? My reply, however cryptic it may seem, will be essentially the same here. First, live in the present as if it were already the future. Second, fear not. A few days later I received a friendly letter from a pastor who had been at my lecture that evening. He asked if I would consider embellishing upon on my answer in my weekly column. (The column happens to appear in the Kansas City diocesan paper.) I promised I would, and I did.

Questions about "strategies for survival" and questions like your own come from that hardy minority of Catholics, mostly women, who are deeply engaged in the life and ministries of the Church: religious educators, social service and healthcare ministers, journalists, teachers, pastors and pastoral associates, and so forth. Unlike most Catholics one finds at Mass on a given weekend, this group of Catholics is directly affected by what is said and done, allowed or prohibited, encouraged or discouraged, by the pope, the Vatican, their bishop, or their pastor. If the lives and ministries of such Catholics are made more demoralized and difficult thereby, they want to know what they can do about it—short of abandoning their ministry or leaving the Church. They don't want to do either.

The first "strategy for survival" I proposed is to live in the present as if it were already the future. For example, women should act now as if their baptismal dignity and ministerial equality were already acknowledged. They should take pastoral initiatives and assume leadership roles that are consistent with their gifts and with the call of their faith-community. True leaders, after all, are people who are trusted and respected by those whom they would lead. Trust and respect, however, aren't conferred by appointment or summoned up on command. Unlike sheer power, leadership is something one earns.

I'm not suggesting that women should preside at clandestine Eucharists before church law allows it (I've already addressed that issue in *Q. 60*, above), but they should do just about everything else short of that. Of course, they will face opposition from unsympathetic clergy, but also from lay people, including other women, who remain wedded to the cultural mentality and religious traditions of the early 20th century.

The second "strategy for survival," however, is as important as the first: fear not. Meaningful change will never happen at the parish level or anywhere else in the Church if we passively accept the way we ourselves and our ministerial roles are defined by others who have never adequately understood, much less fully accepted, the renewal brought about by the Second Vatican Council. Freedom, we must remember, is an interior, spiritual quality. A person under external constraint can still remain an authentically free person, as many unjustly imprisoned people have remained—like Martin Luther King, Jr., or Vaclev Havel, President of the Czech Republic, or St. Paul himself.

The reverse is also true. Although free to come and go as we please, we can be imprisoned nonetheless by a false consciousness that leads us to believe we can't or shouldn't do something that is entirely appropriate for us to do, to believe another has the right to define and determine for us our own human and Christian identity and destiny. The only legitimate fear for a Christian is the fear of God, but in the biblical sense of the word; namely, a readiness to do the will of God. Doing the will of God often requires courage, sometimes even a form of martyrdom. So does living in the present as if the future were already here.

Q. 98. How do you envision the gifts and traditions of others— witness, styles, music, meditation, preaching—being incorporated or adapted by the Church of the future? There seem to be charisms at work outside the Church, even outside Christianity, that are signs of God's work among the human family.

This is one of the most difficult questions to answer because, like most Roman Catholics, I have little or no direct experience of non-Christian and non-Western religious traditions, except for Judaism. I have already pointed out in *Q. 51*, above, that the Second Vatican Council takes a refreshingly catholic (small "c") approach to non-Christian religions. The council's Declaration on the Relationship of the Church to Non-Christian Religions (*Nostra Aetate*) reminds us that God is the one Creator of the whole of the cosmos and of all creatures within it, including ourselves. Variations in religious faith and in the verbal and ritual expression of faith are not a sign of chaos, but rather reflect the rich diversity of God's creative handiwork. Consequently, "The Catholic Church rejects nothing which is true and holy in these religions." Indeed, they "often reflect a ray of that Truth which enlightens all persons" (n. 2). The council, therefore, encouraged "dialogue and collaboration" with the followers of these other religions in order to promote common spiritual and moral values. The document rendered particular respect for Hinduism's emphasis on contemplation, asceticism, and meditation, on Buddhism's sense of detachment from the material world, and on Islam's refined sense of morality and its commitment to prayer, almsgiving, and fasting. So the council clearly agrees with your observation that there seem to be charisms at work even outside of Christianity, as "signs of God's work among the human family."

I don't think there is any question that the impact of these non-Western traditions will be increasingly felt in the Catholic Church of the future. Indeed, the future is already in the making. Many forms of non-Western prayer and meditations have been adopted and adapted for use in Catholic liturgy and devotional practice. Various Eastern spiritual traditions, too, have had a considerable effect on the development of

Catholic spirituality. At the same time, Catholic theologians have turned their attention increasingly to the non-Christian religions. Ecumenism, once confined to inter-Christian dialogue, is now inter-faith. We have moved to what one author has called "the wider ecumenism."

In his 1991 encyclical on the missions, *Redemptoris Missio*, Pope John Paul II commended the path of interreligious dialogue as "a part of the Church's evangelizing mission." "Dialogue," he wrote, "leads to inner purification and conversion, which, if pursued with docility to the Holy Spirit, will be spiritually fruitful."

Q. 99. Will the future changes in our Church depend on who is selected as the next pope?

In large measure, "Yes." But this is not because, according to the will of Christ, the pope is the only one who really counts in the Church. In the present system of church governance—one that has been in effect, more or less, throughout the entire second Christian millennium—the pope is the central human figure in the Church. His theology, his spirituality, his pastoral judgment, his style of leadership are more decisive for the theological, spiritual, pastoral, and governing spirit of the Catholic Church than any other single factor. As I've pointed out earlier, however, that hasn't always been the case—particularly in the first Christian millennium—and it need not be the case in the third.

One of the most common assumptions abroad today, both inside and outside the Catholic Church, is that a pope is always succeeded by a carbon-copy of himself, particularly if his pontificate was long enough to allow for the appointment of many, if not most, of the cardinals who elect his successor. But the history of papal elections refutes this assumption.

Take the last two centuries alone. After one of the longest pontificates in history (1775-99), Pope Pius VI should have been succeeded by a close cardinal-ally. But it took fourteen weeks to break a stalemate and the worldly and extravagant Pius VI was succeeded by a self-effacing Benedictine, Pius VII. After twenty-three years in office, Pius VII, in turn, should have been succeeded by another moderate. Indeed, he had expressed a particular preference before his death, but he was succeeded instead by a conservative, Leo XII, who had been private secretary to the worldly Pius VI. After five and a half years, he was succeeded by yet another moderate, Pius VIII, the one whom Pius VII had hoped would directly succeed him. Pius VIII was succeeded by one of the most reactionary popes in history, Gregory XVI, and, after fifteen years, he was succeeded by a known liberal, who took the name Pius IX. Under pressure of events in Italy, however, Pius IX became very conservative. In spite of having had the longest reign in the entire history of the papacy, Pius IX was succeeded by a moderate, Leo XIII, and not by his conservative secretary of state. And after 25 years, the moderate, Leo XIII, was succeeded by—you guessed it—a conservative, not by *his* moderate secretary of state. And the conservative Pius X by the moderate Benedict XV, and he by the conservative Pius XI. In our own time, the austere Pius XII was succeeded in 1958, after nearly twenty years in office, by the jovial John XXIII, and he by the scholarly Paul VI, and he by the frail and smiling John Paul I, and he by the vigorous and determined John Paul II. And he by...? You get the point, I'm sure.

Q. 100. Do you foresee the possibility of the U.S. Catholic Church breaking away from Rome?

There is always the possibility of anything like that happening, but I believe it to be so remote as to be practically non-existent. If you had asked about the "probability" rather than the "possibility" of a schism in the U.S. Catholic Church, I would have responded with an unequivocal, "No."

This question has been asked many times since the council, and the underlying assumption seems always to be that, if there is going to be a schism in the United States, it will be initiated by liberal Catholics who are unhappy with what they see as a reversal of the reforms of the council by the official leaders of the Church today. What should be remembered, however, is that, since the Second Vatican Council, there has been only one schism in the Catholic Church, and that was a schism on the right, not the left. I refer, of course, to the schism led by the late Archbishop Marcel Lefebvre. A Holy Ghost priest who did missionary work in Africa after ordination in 1929, he became a bishop in 1947 and later served as the Vatican's apostolic delegate for all French-speaking Catholics in Africa. He attended all four sessions of the council, but refused to sign some of its documents. He was especially unhappy with the council's support for ecumenism, the collegiality of bishops, and the Church's social apostolate. In 1970 he opened a so-called traditionalist seminary in Switzerland and moved further and further away from communion with the Bishop of Rome. His vehement and public opposition to the council led to his suspension from the exercise of his priestly and episcopal functions in 1976, but after the election of Pope John Paul II in 1978 there were increased efforts on the part of the Vatican to effect a reconciliation with Lefebvre. The archbishop stubbornly held his ground and the final break came when in 1988 he ordained bishops without authorization from the Holy See, thereby incurring automatic excommunication under canon law. His movement split thereafter into two groups: those who returned to communion with the Bishop of Rome (the Priestly Fraternity of St. Peter) and those who remained with Lefebvre in the Society of St. Pius X. Priest-members of the former group have permission to celebrate the Eucharist according to the preconciliar Tridentine rite.

If there is to be a schism of any kind in the U.S. Catholic Church, it would more likely be initiated by ultra-conservative Catholics in a subsequent, more progressive pontificate than that of John Paul II. But even that is only a possibility, not a probability.

Q. 101. I hear you speaking hopefully about the future of the Catholic Church. Do you have times of personal discouragement and, if so, how do you deal with them?

I always make a distinction between hope and optimism. Hope is a theological virtue; optimism is a human tendency to expect the best outcome or to focus on the most positive aspects of a situation or circumstance. I think it is difficult for Catholics who are firmly committed to the letter and especially to the spirit of the Second Vatican Council to be optimistic about the immediate future of the Catholic Church (that is, the next five to twenty-five years), because all of the *human* signs would indicate that resistance to the council's reforms will continue. Young priests are more conservative than those who are moving toward retirement. The appointment of bishops follows an almost inexorable pattern of movement from moderate to conservative to even more conservative. Very conservative lay movements, like Opus Dei and Comunione e Liberazione (the latter more moderate than the former), and new religious orders, like the Legionaries of Christ, clearly enjoy the special favor of the Holy See. Indeed, the Vatican seems firmly in the hands of those who advance what some have called a restorationist agenda in the Church today. Meanwhile, many thousands of Catholics all over the world, especially women, are either drifting away from active participation in the life of the Church or feeling themselves increasingly alienated from its pastoral leadership. If it were a matter of optimism alone, I would probably be more discouraged than encouraged by developments in the Church today.

But hope is another matter. It is concerned with what is ultimate and eternal, not only with what is immediate and temporal. We hope in God's promises to grant us the gift of eternal life—a life of communion with God and with all of saved humanity. The fulfillment of optimism depends primarily upon our own human efforts; the fulfillment of hope depends ultimately upon God, as well as our own efforts in response to God's grace. To believe in God, to believe in the power of the Holy Spirit, to believe that the Lord will come again to bring all things under his headship is to have hope in the theological sense of the word. No single human event, or pastoral leader, or religious movement can thwart the will and the promises of God to bring good out of evil, to draw all things into eternal glory. St. Paul defined faith as "the assurance of things hoped for" (Heb 11:1). To have faith, therefore, is to have hope.

But I do indeed have many moments of discouragement. I even experience occasional temptations to leave the Church, not because of its central doctrinal and moral teachings about Jesus Christ, redemption, eternal life, love of neighbor, justice, mercy, compassion, forgiveness, but because of the physical and psychic energy one must expend, so needlessly, just to keep at bay fellow Catholics whose understanding of the faith seems almost diametrically opposed to one's own. I am also discouraged by the pain and demoralization I see in so many good people, especially women, who have so much to offer the Church and who want only to serve it in accordance with their own vocation and talents.

But I stay for at least two fundamental reasons: one human, the other spiritual. The first reason is a sense of obligation to the many thousands of Catholics who have written or spoken to me directly over the years to let me know that I give them hope and reason to remain in the Church. At the same time, I have never had a Catholic tell me that she or he left the Church because my words or writings gave them the courage or the excuse to do so. The second reason for staying is faith— the faith that is the foundation of hope. I believe in Jesus Christ. I believe that he is the personification of God. I believe that he represents and embodies humanity at its best—humanity as it is destined to become. I believe that human integrity and fulfillment can only be realized through the values that he proclaimed and lived, even unto death on a cross. My second reason, therefore, is the same as Peter's when he and the other Apostles were confronted by Jesus, "Do you also wish to go away?" And Peter answered, "Lord, to whom can we go? You have the words of eternal life" (John 6:67-68).

In the end, our ultimate loyalty is not to the Church, but to the Reign of God and to Jesus Christ, who alone is "the way, and the truth, and the life" (John 14:6).

BIBLIOGRAPHY

Recommended for Further Reading:

Bokenkotter, Thomas. *A Concise History of the Catholic Church.* Revised and expanded edition. New York: Doubleday Image Books, 1990.

Brown, Raymond E. *The Churches the Apostles Left Behind: New Testament Cradles of Catholic Christianity.* New York: Paulist Press, 1985.

_____. *The Community of the Beloved Disciple: The Life, Loves, and Hates of an Individual Church in New Testament Times.* New York: Paulist Press, 1979.

Brown, Raymond E., et al. *Peter in the New Testament: A Collaborative Assessment by Protestant and Roman Catholic Scholars.* New York: Paulist Press, 1973.

Brown, Raymond E., and John P. Meier, *Antioch and Rome.* New York: Paulist Press, 1983.

Chittister, Joan. *Women, Ministry and Church.* New York: Paulist Press, 1994.

Cwiekowski, Frederick J. *The Beginnings of the Church.* New York: Paulist Press, 1988.

Dulles, Avery. *Models of the Church.* Expanded edition. Garden City, N.Y.: Doubleday Image Books, 1987.

Hastings, Adrian, ed. *Modern Catholicism: Vatican II and After.* New York: Oxford University Press, 1991.

McBrien, Richard P. *Catholicism.* Completely revised and updated edition. San Francisco: HarperCollins, 1994.

_____, general editor. *The HarperCollins Encyclopedia of Catholicism*. San Francisco: HarperCollins, 1995.

_____. *Ministry: A Theological, Pastoral Handbook*. San Francisco: Harper & Row, 1987.

Osborne, Kenan R. *Ministry: Lay Ministry in the Roman Catholic Church: Its History and Theology*. New York: Paulist Press, 1993.

O'Meara, Thomas F. *Theology of Ministry*. New York: Paulist Press, 1983.

Sullivan, Francis A. *The Church We Believe In: One, Holy, Catholic and Apostolic*. New York: Paulist Press, 1988.

_____. *Magisterium: Teaching Authority in the Catholic Church*. New York: Paulist Press, 1983.

Tillard, Jean-M. R. *The Bishop of Rome*. Wilmington, Del.: Michael Glazier, 1983.

INDEX OF SUBJECTS TREATED
IN THE QUESTIONS

(The numbers listed below *refer to Questions*, not to pages.)

Other Books in the Series

RESPONSES TO 101 QUESTIONS ON THE BIBLE
by Raymond E. Brown, S.S.

RESPONSES TO 101 QUESTIONS ON THE
DEAD SEA SCROLLS
by Joseph A. Fitzmyer, S.J.

RESPONSES TO 101 QUESTIONS ABOUT JESUS
by Michael L. Cook, S.J.

RESPONSES TO 101 QUESTIONS ABOUT FEMINISM
by Denise Lardner Carmody

RESPONSES TO 101 QUESTIONS ON THE
PSALMS AND OTHER WRITINGS
by Roland E. Murphy, O. Carm.

RESPONSES TO 101 QUESTIONS ON THE
BIBICAL TORAH
by Roland E. Murphy, O. Carm.